SEXUAL HARASSMENT

SEXUAL HARASSMENT

KNOW YOUR RIGHTS!

MARTIN ESKENAZI
AND DAVID GALLEN

Carroll & Graf Publishers, Inc.
New York

First Carroll & Graf edition 1992

Carroll & Graf Publishers, Inc.
260 Fifth Avenue
New York, NY 10001

Library of Congress Cataloging-in-Publication Data is available.

ISBN: 0-88184-816-6

Manufactured in the United States of America

To my parents, Sam and Joni, and
my brothers, Gregg and Jay,
the greatest family one could ever have.

Acknowledgments

I would like to thank Richard and Dave Gallen for their insight and extensive contributions. Without them this book would not have been possible.

I also wish to thank Ayesha Khan for her friendship and constant support, which extends well beyond the time it took to put this book together.

—Martin Eskenazi

Permissions

The publisher gratefully acknowledges permission to reprint from the following:

NOW Legal Defense and Education Fund for the NOW LDEF Legal Resource Kit on Employment.

University of Southern California Law Review for "The Nature of the Beast" (*Southern California Law Review*, Vol. 65, 1992).

Yale University Press for Chapter 3 of *Sexual Harassment of Working Women* by Professor Catherine MacKinnon (Yale University Press, 1979) © 1979 by Yale University Press.

Contents

	Preface	9
Chapter 1	"The Nature of the Beast" by Anita Hill	11
Chapter 2	"Sexual Harassment: The Experience" by Catherine MacKinnon	17
Chapter 3	Questions and Answers	61
Chapter 4	NOW Legal Resource Kit	119
Chapter 5	EEOC Guidelines	159
Chapter 6	Resources and Bibliography	190
	Index	215

Preface

Sexual harassment is by definition unwelcome attention. It is also illegal. There are ways to protect yourself against sexual harassment. To do so requires a knowledge of the laws regarding sexual harassment and the remedies available to you. It is our hope that this book will provide you with the knowledge, the knowhow and the inspiration to stand fast against sexual harassment and any other form of sexual exploitation.

—The Authors

Chapter 1

The Nature Of the Beast

by Anita Hill

The response to my Senate Judiciary Committee testimony has been at once heartwarming and heart-wrenching. In learning that I am not alone in experiencing harassment, I am also learning that there are far too many women who have experienced a range of inexcusable and illegal activities—from sexist jokes to sexual assault—on the job.

My reaction has been to try to learn more. As an educator, I always begin to study an issue by examining the scientific data—the articles, the books, the studies. Perhaps the most compelling lesson is in the stories told by the women who have written to me. I have learned much; I am continuing to learn; I have yet ten times as much to explore. I want to share some of this with you.

"The Nature of the Beast" describes the existence of sexual harassment, which is alive and well. A harmful, dangerous thing that can confront a woman at any time.

What we know about harassment, sizing up the beast:

Sexual harassment is pervasive.

1. It occurs today at an alarming rate. Statistics show that anywhere from 42 to 90 percent of women will experience some form of harassment during their employed lives. At least one percent experience sexual assault. But the statistics do not fully tell

the story of the anguish of women who have been told in various ways on the first day of a job that sexual favors are expected. Or the story of women who were sexually assaulted by men with whom they continued to work.

2. It has been occurring for years. In letters to me, women tell of incidents that occurred 50 years ago when they were first entering the workplace, incidents they have been unable to speak of for that entire period.

3. Harassment crosses lines of race and class. In some ways, it is a creature that practices "equal opportunity" where women are concerned. In other ways it exhibits predictable prejudices and reflects stereotypical myths held by our society.

We know that harassment all too often goes unreported for a variety of reasons.

1. Unwillingness (for good reason) to deal with the expected consequences.

2. Self-blame.

3. Threats or blackmail by co-workers or employers.

4. What it boils down to in many cases is a sense of powerlessness that we experience in the workplace, and our acceptance of a certain level of inability to control our careers and professional destinies. This sense of powerlessness is particularly troubling when one observes the research that says individuals with graduate education experience more harassment than do persons with less than a high school diploma. The message: when you try to obtain power through education, the beast harassment responds by striking more often and more vehemently.

That harassment is treated like a woman's "dirty secret" is well known. We also know what happens when we "tell." We know that when harassment is reported the common reaction is disbelief or worse.

1. Women who "tell" lose their jobs. A typical response told of in the letters to me was: I not only lost my job for reporting harassment, but I was accused of stealing and charges were brought against me.

2. Women who "tell" become emotionally wasted. One writer noted that "it was fully eight months after the suit was conducted that I began to see myself as alive again."

3. Women who "tell" are not always supported by other women. Perhaps the most disheartening stories I have received are of mothers not believing daughters. In my kindest moments I believe that this reaction only represents attempts to distance ourselves from the pain of the harassment experience. The internal response is: "It didn't happen to me. This couldn't happen to me. In order to believe that I am protected, I must believe that it didn't happen to her." The external response is: "What did you do to provoke that kind of behavior?" Yet at the same time that I have been advised of hurtful and unproductive reactions, I have also heard stories of mothers and daughters sharing their experiences. In some cases the sharing allows for a closer bonding. In others a slight but cognizable mending of a previously damaged relationship occurs.

What we are learning about harassment requires recognizing this beast when we encounter it, and more. It requires looking the beast in the eye.

We are learning painfully that simply having laws against harassment on the books is not enough. The law, as it was conceived, was to provide a shield of protection for us. Yet that shield is failing us: many fear reporting, others feel it would do no good. The result is that less than 5 percent of women victims file claims of harassment. Moreover, the law focuses on quid pro quo, but a recent *New York Times* article quoting psychologist Dr. Louise Fitzgerald says that this makes up considerably less than 5 percent of the cases. The law needs to be more responsive to the reality of our experiences.

As we are learning, enforcing the law alone won't terminate the problem. What we are seeking is equality of treatment in the workplace. Equality requires an expansion of our attitudes toward workers. Sexual harassment denies our treatment as equals and replaces it with treatment of women as objects of ego or power gratification. Dr. John Gottman, a psychologist at the University of Washington, notes that sexual harassment is more about fear than about sex.

Yet research suggests two troublesome responses exhibited by workers and by courts. Both respond by:

1. Downplaying the seriousness of the behavior (seeing it as

normal sexual attraction between people) or commenting on the sensitivity of the victim.

2. Exaggerating the ease with which victims are expected to handle the behavior. But my letters tell me that unwanted advances do not cease—and that the message was power, not genuine interest.

We are learning that many women are angry. The reasons for the anger are various and perhaps all too obvious.

1. We are angry because this awful thing called harassment exists in terribly harsh, ugly, demeaning, and even debilitating ways. Many believe it is criminal and should be punished as such. It is a form of violence against women as well as a form of economic coercion, and our experiences suggest that it won't just go away.

2. We are angry because for a brief moment we believed that if the law allowed for women to be hired in the workplace, and if we worked hard for our educations and on the job, equality would be achieved. We believed we would be respected as equals. Now we are realizing this is not true. We have been betrayed. The reality is that this powerful beast is used to perpetuate a sense of inequality, to keep women in their place notwithstanding our increasing presence in the workplace.

What we have yet to explore about harassment is vast. It is what will enable us to slay the beast.

Research is helpful, appreciated, and I hope will be required reading for all legislators. Yet research has what I see as one shortcoming: it focuses on our reaction to harassment, not on the harasser. How we enlighten men who are currently in the workplace about behavior that is beneath our (and their) dignity is the challenge of the future. Research shows that men tend to have a narrower definition of what constitutes harassment than do women. How do we expand their body of knowledge? How do we raise a generation of men who won't need to be reeducated as adults? We must explore these issues, and research efforts can assist us.

What are the broader effects of harassment on women and the world? Has sexual harassment left us unempowered? Has our potential in the workplace been greatly damaged by this beast? Has this form of economic coercion worked? If so, how do we begin to reverse its effects? We must begin to use what we know to move to the next step: what we will do about it.

How do we capture our rage and turn it into positive energy? Through the power of women working together, whether it be in the political arena, or in the context of a lawsuit, or in community service. This issue goes well beyond partisan politics. Making the workplace a safer, more productive place for ourselves and our daughters should be on the agenda for each of us. It is something we can do for ourselves. It is a tribute, as well, to our mothers—and indeed a contribution we can make to the entire population.

I wish that I could take each of you on the journey that I've been on during all these weeks since the hearing. I wish that every one of you could experience the heartache and the triumphs of each of those who have shared with me their experiences. I leave you with but a brief glimpse of what I've seen. I hope it is enough to encourage you to begin—or continue and persist with—your own exploration. And thank you.

This article is based on remarks delivered by Anita Hill (professor of law, University of Oklahoma) as part of a panel on sexual harassment and policymaking at the National Forum for Women State Legislators convened by the Center for the American Woman and Politics (CAWP) in late 1991. Other panel members were Deborah L. Rhode, professor of law at Stanford; Susan Deller Ross, professor of law and director of the Sex Discrimination Clinic at Georgetown University Law School; and Kimberle Williams Crenshaw, professor of law at UCLA. A transcript of the entire proceedings (the largest meeting of elected women ever held) is available from CAWP, Eagleton Institute of Politics, Rutgers University, New Brunswick, New Jersey 08901.

Chapter 2

Sexual Harassment:
The Experience

by Catherine MacKinnon

Most women wish to choose whether, when, where, and with whom to have sexual relationships, as one important part of exercising control over their lives. Sexual harassment denies this choice in the process of denying the opportunity to study or work without being subjected to sexual exactions. Objection to sexual harassment at work is not a neopuritan moral protest against signs of attraction, displays of affection, compliments, flirtation, or touching on the job. Instead, women

are rattled and often angry about sex that is one-sided, unwelcome or comes with strings attached. When it's something a woman wants to turn off but can't (a co-worker or supervisor who refuses to stop) or when it's coming from someone with the economic power to hire or fire, help or hinder, reward or punish (an employer or client who mustn't be offended)—that's when [women] say it's a problem.[1]

Women who protest sexual harassment at work are resisting economically enforced sexual exploitation.

Sexual Harassment: The Experience

This chapter* analyzes sexual harassment as women report experiencing it.[2] The analysis is necessarily preliminary and exploratory. These events have seldom been noticed, much less studied; they have almost never been studied *as* sexual harassment.[3] Although the available material is limited, it covers a considerably broader range of incidents than courts will (predictably) consider to be sex discrimination. Each incident or facet of the problem mentioned here will not have equal *legal* weight or go to the same legal issue; not every instance or aspect of undesired sexual attention on the job is necessarily part of the legal cause of action. Some dimensions of the problem seem to contraindicate legal action or to require determinations that courts are ill suited to make. The broader contextual approach is taken to avoid prematurely making women's experience of sexual harassment into a case of sex discrimination, no more and no less. For it is, at times, both more and less.

I envision a two-way process of interaction between the relevant legal concepts and women's experience. The strictures of the concept of sex discrimination will ultimately constrain those aspects of women's oppression that will be legally recognized as discriminatory. At the same time, women's experiences, expressed in their own way, can push to expand that concept. Such an approach not only enriches the law. It begins to shape it so that what *really* happens to women, not some male vision of what happens to women, is at the core of the legal prohibition. Women's lived-through experience, in as whole and truthful a fashion as can be approximated at this point, should begin to provide the starting point and context out of which is constructed the narrower forms of abuse that will be made illegal on their behalf. Now that a few women have the tools to address the legal system on its own terms, the law can begin to address women's experience on women's own terms.[4]

Although the precise extent and contours of sexual harassment await further and more exacting investigation, preliminary research indicates that the problem is extremely widespread. Certainly it is more common than almost anyone thought. In the pio-

* from Catherine MacKinnon, *Sexual Harassment and Working Women,* Yale University Press, 1979.

neering survey by Working Women United Institute,[5] out of a sample of 55 food service workers and 100 women who attended a meeting on sexual harassment, from five to seven of every ten women reported experiencing sexual harassment in some form at some time in their work lives. Ninety-two percent of the total sample thought it a serious problem. In a study of all women employed at the United Nations, 49 percent said that sexual pressure currently existed on their jobs.[6] During the first eight months of 1976, the Division of Human Rights of the State of New York received approximately 45 complaints from women alleging sexual harassment on the job.[7] Of 9,000 women who responded voluntarily to a questionnaire in *Redbook Magazine,* "How do you handle sex on the job?" nine out of ten reported experiences of sexual harassment. Of course, those who experience the problem may be most likely to respond. Nevertheless, before this survey, it would have been difficult to convince a person of ordinary skepticism that 8,100 American women existed who would report experiencing sexual harassment at work.

Using the *Redbook* questionnaire, a naval officer found 81 percent of a sample of women on a navy base and in a nearby town reported employment-related sexual harassment in some form.[8] These frequency figures must, of course, be cautiously regarded. But even extrapolating conservatively, given that nine out of ten American women work outside the home some time in their lives[9] and that in April 1974, 45 percent of American women sixteen and over, or 35 million women, were employed in the labor force,[10] it is clear that a lot of women are potentially affected. As the problem begins to appear structural rather than individual, *Redbook*'s conclusion that "the problem is not epidemic; it is pandemic—an everyday, everywhere occurrence"[11] does not seem incredible.

One need not show that sexual harassment is commonplace in order to argue that it is severe for those afflicted, or even that it is sex discrimination. However, if one shows that sexual harassment in employment systematically occurs between the persons and under the conditions that an analysis of it as discrimination suggests—that is, as a function of sex as gender—one undercuts the view that it occurs because of some unique chemistry between particular (or aberrant) individuals. That sexual harassment does occur to a large and diverse population of women supports an analysis that it occurs *because* of their group characteristic, that is, sex. Such a showing supports an analysis of the abuse as structural, and as such, worth legal attention as sex discrimination, not just as unfairness between two individuals, which might better be approached through private law.

If the problem is so common, one might ask why it has not been commonly analyzed or protested. Lack of public information, social awareness, and formal data probably reflects less its exceptionality than its specific pathology. Sexual subjects are generally sensitive and considered private; women feel embarrassed, demeaned, and intimidated by these incidents.[12] They feel afraid, despairing, utterly alone, and complicit. This is not the sort of experience one discusses readily. Even more to the point, sexual advances are often accompanied by threats of retaliation if exposed. Revealing these pressures enough to protest them thus risks the very employment consequences which sanctioned the advances in the first place.

It is not surprising either that women would not complain of an experience for which there has been no name. Until 1976,[13] lacking a term to express it, sexual harassment was literally unspeakable, which made a generalized, shared, and social definition of it inaccessible. The unnamed should not be mistaken for the nonexistent. Silence often speaks of pain and degradation so thorough that the situation cannot be conceived as other than it is:

When the conception of change is beyond the limits of the possible, there are no words to articulate discontent, so it is sometimes held not to exist. This mistaken belief arises because we can only grasp silence in the moment in which it is breaking. The sound of silence breaking makes us understand what we could not hear before. But the fact we could not hear does not prove that no pain existed.[14]

As Adrienne Rich has said of this kind of silence, "Do not mistake it/for any kind of absence."[15] Until very recently issues analogous to sexual harassment, such as abortion, rape, and wife beating existed at the level of an open secret in public consciousness, supporting the (equally untrue) inference that these events were infrequent as well as shameful, and branding the victim with the stigma of deviance. In light of these factors, more worth explaining is the emergence of women's ability to break the silence.

Victimization by the practice of sexual harassment, so far as is currently known, occurs across the lines of age, marital status, physical appearance, race, class, occupation, pay range, and any other factor that distinguishes women from each other.[16] Frequency and type of incident may vary with specific vulnerabilities of the woman, or qualities of the job, employer, situation, or workplace, to an extent so far undetermined. To this point, the common denominator is that the perpetrators tend to be men, the victims women. Most of the perpetrators are employment superiors, although some are co-workers or clients. Of the 155 women in the Working Women United Institute sample, 40 percent were harassed by a male superior, 22 percent by a co-worker, 29 percent by a client, customer, or person who had no direct working relationship with them; 1 percent were harassed by a subordinate and 8 percent by "other."[17]

As to age and marital status, *Redbook* finds the most common story is of a woman in her twenties fending off a boss in his sixties, someone she would never choose as a sexual partner. The majority of women who responded to the survey, in which 92 percent reported incidents of sexual harassment, were in their twenties or thirties, and married. Adultery seems no deterrent. However, many women were single or formerly married and ranged in age from their teens to their sixties. In the Working Women United Institute speak-out, one woman mentioned an incident that occurred when she was working as a child model at age ten; another reported an experience at age 55.[18] The women in that sample ranged in age from 19 to 61. On further investigation, sexual harassment as a system may be found to affect women differentially by age, although it damages women regardless of age. That is, many older women may be excluded from jobs because they are considered unattractive sex objects, in order that younger women can be hired to be so treated. But many women preface their reports of sexual harassment with evaluations of their appearance such as, "I am fat and forty, but . . ."[19]

Sexual harassment takes both verbal and physical forms. In

the Working Women United Institute sample, approximately a third of those who reported sexual harassment reported physical forms, nearly two-thirds verbal forms.[20] Verbal sexual harassment can include anything from passing but persistent comments on a woman's body or body parts to the experience of an eighteen-year-old file clerk whose boss regularly called her in to his office "to tell me the intimate details of his marriage and to ask what I thought about different sexual positions."[21] Pornography is sometimes used.[22] Physical forms range from repeated collisions that leave the impression of "accident" to outright rape. One woman reported unmistakable sexual molestation which fell between these extremes: "My boss . . . runs his hand up my leg or blouse. He hugs me to him and then tells me that he is 'just naturally affectionate.' "[23]

There is some suggestion in the data that working class women encounter physical as well as verbal forms of sexual harassment more often than middle class and/or professional women, who more often encounter only the verbal forms.[24] However, women's class status in the strict sense is often ambiguous. Is a secretary for a fancy law firm in a different class from a secretary for a struggling, small business? Is a nurse married to a doctor "working class" or "middle class" on her job? Is a lesbian factory worker from an advantaged background with a rich ex-husband who refuses to help support the children because of her sexual preference "upper class"? In any case, most women who responded to the *Redbook* survey, like most employed women, were working at white collar jobs earning between $5,000 and $10,000 a year. Many more were blue collar, professional, or managerial workers earning less than $5,000 or more than $25,000 a year. They report harassment by men independent of the class of those men.

The Working Women United Institute sample, in which approximately 70 percent reported incidents of sexual harassment, presented a strikingly typical profile of women's employment history. Almost all of the women had done office work of some kind in their work life. A quarter had done sales, a quarter had been teachers, a third file clerks, 42 percent had been either secretaries or receptionists, and 29 percent had done factory work. Currently, 55 percent were food service workers with the remainder scattered among a variety of occupations. The average income was $101–$125 per week. This is very close to, or a little below, the usual weekly earnings of most working women.[25]

Race is an important variable in sexual harassment in several different senses. Black women's reports of sexual harassment by white male superiors reflect a sense of impunity that resounds of slavery and colonization. Maxine Munford,* recently separated and with two children to support, claimed that on the first day at her new job she was asked by her employer "if she would make love to a white man, and if she would slap his face if he made a pass at her." She repeatedly refused such advances and was soon fired, the employer alleging she had inadequate knowledge and training for the job and lacked qualifications. His last statement before she left was: "If you would have intercourse with me seven days a week I might give you your job back."[26] Apparently, sexual harassment can be both a sexist way to express racism and a racist way to express sexism. However, black women also report sexual harassment by black men and white women complain of sexual harassment by black male superiors and co-workers. One complaint for slander and outrageous conduct accused the defendants of making statements including the following:

warning customers about plaintiff's alleged desire to "get in his pants," pointing out that plaintiff had large breasts, stating "Anything over a handful is wasted," calling plaintiff "Momma Fuller" and "Big Momma," referring to her breasts, "Doesn't she have nice (or large) breasts?" "Watch out, she's very horny. She hasn't gotten any lately" "Have you ever seen a black man's penis?" "Do you know how large a black man's penis is?" "Have you ever slept with a black man?" "Do you want to stop the car and screw in the middle of the street?"[27]

One might consider whether white women more readily perceive themselves as *sexually* degraded, or anticipate a supportive response when they complain, when they are sexually harassed by a black man than by a white man. Alternatively, some white women

---

* Her lawsuit, *Munford v. James T. Barnes & Co.*, 441 F. Supp. 459 (E.D. Mich. 1977), is discussed in chapter 4, *Sexual Harassment*, at 73 ff.

confide that they have consciously resisted reporting severe sexual harassment by black men to authorities because they feel the response would be supportive for racist reasons. Although racism is deeply involved in sexual harassment, the element common to these incidents is that the perpetrators are male, the victims female. Few women are in a position to harass men sexually, since they do not control men's employment destinies at work,[28] and female sexual initiative is culturally repressed in this society.[29]

As these experiences suggest, the specific injury of sexual harassment arises from the nexus between a sexual demand and the workplace. Anatomized, the situations can be seen to include a sexual incident or advance, some form of compliance or rejection, and some employment consequence. Sometimes these elements are telescoped, sometimes greatly attenuated, sometimes absent. All are variable: the type of incident or advance, the form of response, and the kind and degree of damage attributable to it.

The critical issues in assessing sexual harassment as a legal cause of action—the issues that need to be explored in light of women's experiences—center upon the definition of and the relationship among three events: the advance, the response, and the employment consequence. Critical questions arise in conceptualizing all three. Where is the line between a sexual advance and a friendly gesture? How actively must the issue be forced? If a woman complies, should the legal consequences be different than if she refuses? Given the attendant risks, how explicitly must a woman reject? Might quitting be treated the same as firing under certain circumstances? To get legal relief, must a job benefit be shown to be merited independent of a sexual bargain, or is the situation an injury in itself? When a perpetrator insists that a series of touchings were not meant to be sexual, but the victim experienced them as unambiguously sexual, assuming both are equally credible, whose interpretation controls when the victim's employment status is damaged? In addressing these questions, it is important to divide matters of persuasion from issues of fact, and both of these from issues which go to the core of the legal concept of the discrimination. The first distinguishes the good from the less good case; the second sets a standard of proof; the third draws a line between a legal claim and no claim at all.

Women's experiences of sexual harassment can be divided into two forms which merge at the edges and in the world. The first I term the *quid pro quo,* in which sexual compliance is exchanged, or proposed to be exchanged, for an employment opportunity. The second arises when sexual harassment is a persistent *condition of work.* This distinction highlights different facets of the problem as women live through it and suggests slightly different legal requirements. In both types, the sexual demand is often but an extension of a gender-defined work role. The victim is employed, hence treated, "as a woman." In the quid pro quo, the woman must comply sexually or forfeit an employment opportunity. The quid pro quo arises most powerfully within the context of horizontal segregation, in which women are employed in feminized jobs, such as office work, as a part of jobs vertically stratified by sex, with men holding the power to hire and fire women. In a job which is defined according to gender, noncompliance with all of the job's requirements, which may at the boss's whim come to include sexual tolerance or activity, operatively "disqualifies" a woman for the job. In sexual harassment as a condition of work, the exchange of sex for employment opportunities is less direct. The major question is whether the *advances themselves* constitute an injury in employment.

QUID PRO QUO

This category is defined by the more or less explicit exchange: the woman must comply sexually or forfeit an employment benefit. The exchange can be anything but subtle, although its expression can be euphemistic: "If I wasn't going to sleep with him, I wasn't going to get my promotion";[30] "I think he meant that I had a job if I played along";[31] "You've got to make love to get a day off or to get a good beat";[32] "[Her] foreman told her that if she wanted the job she would have to be 'nice' ";[33] "I was fired because I refused to give at the office."[34]

Assuming there has been an unwanted sexual advance, a resulting quid pro quo can take one of three possible shapes. In situation one, the woman declines the advance and forfeits an

26

employment opportunity. If the connections are shown, this raises the clearest pattern: sexual advance, noncompliance, employment retaliation. In situation two, the woman complies and does not receive a job benefit. This is complex: was the job benefit denied independently of the sexual involvement? Is employment-coerced sex an injury in itself or does compliance mean consent? Should the woman in effect forfeit the job opportunity as relief *because* she complied sexually? In situation three, the woman complies and receives a job benefit. Does she have an injury to complain of? Do her competitors? In a fourth logical possibility, which does not require further discussion, the woman refuses to comply, receives completely fair treatment on the job, and is never harassed again (and is, no doubt, immensely relieved). In this one turn of events, there truly is "no harm in asking."[35]

In situation one, the injurious nexus is between the imposition of the sexual requirement and the employment retaliation following upon its rejection. To date, all of the legally successful suits for sexual harassment* have alleged some form of the trilogy of unwanted advances, rejection, retaliation. In Adrienne Tomkins's case** the advances occurred over a lunch that was to include a discussion of her upcoming promotion. She refused to comply, was threatened, demoted, and eventually terminated.[36] In the case of Paulette Barnes,† her supervisor repeatedly insisted that she engage in social and sexual activity with him. When she refused, he took away her duties and eventually abolished her position. A witness in Barnes's case described a classic situation of this type in her own experience with the same man:

Q. Did you ever have any problems working under Mr. Z?
The Witness: Well, the problem started when I took a trip to Puerto Rico with Mr. Z in February of 1971. When we got back he took all of my secretarial duties and gave them to E—— M——, who was white. Some-

---

* These cases are discussed in detail in chapter 4, *Sexual Harassment*.
** Her lawsuit is reported as *Tomkins v. Public Service Electric & Gas Co.*, 422 F. Supp. 553 (D. N. J. 1977) reversed on appeal, 568 F.2d 1044 (3rd Cir. 1977), discussed in chapter 4, *ibid.* at 69–72.
† Her lawsuit is reported as *Barnes v. Castle*, 561 F.2d 983 (D.C. Cir. 1977), discussed in chapter 4, *ibid.* at 65–68.

thing happened in Puerto Rico, and he used to write me nasty little notes and things like that.

By Miss Barnes:‡

Q. Could you tell us exactly what happened in Puerto Rico or is this confidential information?

A. Well, when we went to Puerto Rico, I was going there as his secretary to take notes on the conferences. . . . When we got there he was supposed to make hotel reservations. He took that out of my hands and when we got there he didn't do it. We waited around until 10:00 or 11:00 that night to get a hotel.

When we got there we went upstairs and put our bags in the room. His bags were in the room, so, he said he had to go and take someone to another hotel, and he would be back to get his things.

When he came back he started undressing, and I told him that he could not stay in the same room with me. He asked me why, and I said—

Mr. H——: (attorney for Mr. Z) I think we get the picture.

Appeals Examiner: There was a dispute over room accommodations. Is this one of the problems?

The Witness: Right.

Appeals Examiner: You came back and then what happened?

The Witness: He started writing me nasty little notes telling me he no longer wanted me to work for him. He started giving all of his duties to E —— instead of me, and he even asked me to quit working for him because of what happened.[37]

This structure was also presented in *Alexander v. Yale,* a case complaining of sexual harassment in education. A student who refused a professor's advances allegedly received a low grade in a course.[38] In a related situation, a woman who declined to "join [her employer] in his bed" while on a business trip was reminded at lunch the next day that she was soon to be reviewed for reappointment, that her chances depended largely upon his support and recommendation, and that she would be well served if she "linked both her professional work and her personal life more closely to his own needs." She did not do so. Subsequently she was not renewed, a decision in which his lack of support and negative recommendation were instrumental. He stated publicly that in his decision he regretfully recognized the fact that they had not been

‡ Ms. Barnes was not represented by counsel at this point in the proceedings.

able to establish "a closer personal relationship." Women commonly report such a man's insistence that a sexual relationship is essential to their working relationship[39] and that without it the women cannot maintain their jobs.

Some employers use job sanctions to promote the sexual harassment of their female employees by male customers or clients, as well as to assure their own sexual access, and to punish the noncompliant:

June, a waitress in Arkansas, was serving a customer when he reached up her skirt. When she asked her manager for future protection against such incidents, she was harassed by him instead. "They put me on probation," she recalled, "as if I was the guilty one. Then things went from bad to worse. I got lousy tables and bad hours."[40]

In each case, following the woman's refusal, the man retaliated through use of his power over her job or career. Retaliation comes in many forms. The woman may be threatened with demotions and salary cuts; unfavorable material may be solicited and put in her personal file; or she may be placed on disciplinary layoff.[41] In one case, a sexually disappointed foreman first cut back the woman's hours, then put her on a lower-paying machine. When she requested extra work to make up the difference, he put her to sweeping floors and cleaning bathrooms. He degraded and ridiculed her constantly, interfered with her work so it was impossible for her to maintain production, and fired her at two o'clock one morning.[42] In another case, failing to extract sexual favors, the supervisor belittled the woman, stripped her of her job duties, and then abolished her job.[43] In another, a supervisor, following rejection of his elaborate sexual advances, barraged the woman with unwarranted reprimands about her job performance, refused routine supervision or task direction, which made it impossible for her to do her job, and then fired her for poor work performance.[44]

Sudden allegations of job incompetence and poor attitude commonly follow rejection of sexual advances and are used to support employment consequences. When accused of sexual harassment, men often respond that they were only trying to initiate a close personal relationship with a woman they liked very much. In

Margaret Miller's situation,* her superior at the bank appeared at her door, bottle in hand, saying, "I've never felt this way about a black chick before."[45] Women who refuse become just as abruptly disliked. In this case, the bank stated that the reason for Ms. Miller's firing was her "insubordination to Mr. Taufer."[46] Under parallel factual circumstances, one judge pointedly concluded: "Ms. Elliott was not terminated because of . . . her insubordination except such insubordination as was embodied in her refusal to go along with Lawler's propositions."†[47]

Women whose work had been praised and encouraged suddenly find themselves accused of incompetence or of sabotaging their employer's projects and blamed for any downturn in business fortunes. The investigator in Diane Williams's case* was suspicious:

How did an employee hired in January suddenly become so bad that during the period from July 17 through September 11, a case was built for her separation? . . . I believe a program of faultfinding, criticism and documentation of minor offenses was undertaken.[48]

Some employers do not even bother to create the appearance of actual job incompetence:

The man who was second in command to my boss asked me out and I fielded it. I was charming but I said no. He said that I'd be sorry. . . . Later on, my boss said he had evidence of my inefficiency on which he could fire me, and when I said it wasn't possible, he said he would make evidence. He was supported by the man who had asked me out.[49]

Situation two, the second of the three forms of the quid pro quo, requires inquiry into the impact of compliance. Even less is known about women who comply than about those who refuse. But there is little to suggest that women who meet sexual conditions receive job benefits. More common is the following: "I'm told

* Her lawsuit is reported as *Miller v. Bank of America*, 418 F. Supp. 233 (N.D. Cal. 1976), *appeal pending*, discussed in chapter 4, *ibid*. at 61–63.
† Sherry Elliott's lawsuit, *Elliott v. Emery Air Freight*, is unreported; it is discussed in chapter 4, *ibid*. at 72–73.
* Diane Williams's case is reported as *Williams v. Saxbe*, 413 F. Supp. 654 (D.D.C. 1976) and is discussed in chapter 4. *ibid*. at 63–65.

by the supervisors that the women on the oil slopes and in the camps are fired if they do and also fired if they don't."[50] This suggests that employment sanctions simultaneously prohibit and compel compliance with employment-related sexual advances. Women both must and may not comply—or face the consequences. Constantina Safilios-Rothschild suggests one possible explanation for men's failure to deliver promised job rewards:

Actually it has been quite questionable whether women did in fact obtain economic security through marriage, or desirable occupational advancement in exchange for sexual favors. In the latter case, most often adulterous men, for a variety of motivations (including guilt and fear that their infidelity will be suspected or known) have not returned favors or have done very little. Others have simply not honored the existence of any self-understood or implicit contract of exchange of favors.[51]

This implies that men believe that whenever women are advanced on the job, an exchange of sexual favors must have occurred.

If such a compact were made and broken, a woman attempting to get the benefit of her bargain would encounter little sympathy and probably less legal support. But this misconstrues the issue. Whether or not the woman complies, the crucial issue is whether she was sexually coerced by economic threats or promises. Requiring her to decline would allow the employer to impose such a deal in bad faith, secure sexual favors, and then assert she had no right to complain because she had done what he had no right to demand. Her compliance does not mean it is not still blackmail. Nevertheless, allowing a compliant woman to sue for sexual harassment when an exchange fails leaves open the unattractive possibility of encouraging women to acquiesce in unwanted sex for purposes of career advancement, knowing that they can enforce the man's promise if he does not perform as agreed. For this reason (among others) it would seem preferable to define the injury of sexual harassment as the injury of being *placed in the position* of having to choose between unwanted sex and employment benefits or favorable conditions. From the standpoint of proof, situation two would then make a woman's case weaker (although not impossible) than before she complied. It would simply undercut the plausibility of the argument that her advancement was contingent upon compliance. Such a posture would support women in refusing unwanted sex, and discourage abuse of the cause of action through attempts to get whatever could be gained through sexual compliance and reserving legal resort for times when it did not work out.

"The other side" of sexual harassment is commonly thought to be raised by situation three, in which women who comply with sexual conditions are advantaged in employment over men or over women who refuse. Despite the indications that few benefits redound to the woman who accedes, much folklore exists about the woman who "slept her way to the top" or the academic professional woman who "got her degree on her back." These aphorisms suggest that women who are not qualified for their jobs or promotions acquire them instead by sexual means. Do these stories raise serious difficulties for a conceptualization of sexual harassment as integral to women's employment *dis*advantagement?[52]

Since so few women get to the top at all, it cannot be very common for them to get there by sexual means. Yet undoubtedly some individuals, whether by calculation or in the face of discrimination and lack of recognition of their qualifications, must have followed this course. A mix of these elements is suggested in the following (undocumented) observation: "By using sex, women were able to diminish the social distance between important, rich or powerful men and themselves, and to obtain desirable goods such as economic security and social status through marriage, or a desirable job or promotion through sexual relations with an influential man."[53] Although the author of this statement qualifies it substantially in a footnote, she concludes: "There are, however, even at present a few outstanding examples of professional women, businesswomen, and artists whose occupational success is largely due to a powerful male with whom they have a long-standing and open relationship."[54] This portrays a relationship that appears more like a consensual one than like unwanted sex acquiesced in for career advancement, although it is admittedly difficult to tell the difference.

As discussed earlier, women consistently occupy the lowest-status, lowest-paying jobs, much lower than men of the same education and experience. Given this, it is difficult to argue that women in general receive advantages even remotely comparable with the sexual harassment to which they are subjected. This, after all, is the implication of the supposed "other side": some women are hurt by the practice, it is said, but then look at all the women who benefit from it. Initially, it seems worth asking, as a hypothetical parallel, whether if some blacks are advantaged just because they are black, that is a reason why blacks who are disadvantaged because they are black should continue to be. Next, from the available data on sex discrimination, it cannot be deduced that women in general (and certainly not in individual cases) derive undeserved job opportunities from sexual compliance or by any other means. On the contrary, it would be difficult to show that cooperating women derive advantages commensurate even with the disadvantage of being female. Of course, it is impossible to estimate how much worse women's position might be without the possible contribution of unwanted sex to their side of the bargain. Overall, however, the statistics on discrimination suggest that no fulfillment of any requirement, sexual demands included, results in job status for which women are qualified, much less undeserved advancement.

Presuming for the argument that these stories have some truth, one might look at women who "succeed" this way as having extricated themselves from a situation of sexual harassment. Rather than deriving unfair advantages because of their sex, perhaps they had to meet unfair requirements because of their sex. In this perspective, the woman who "slept her way to the top" may have been the woman who would not have been hired or promoted, regardless of qualifications, without fulfilling sexual conditions, conditions equally qualified men do not have to fulfill. Moreover, for every woman who "got her degree on her back," there were men who offered rewards, supervision, and attention to her development only at a sexual price. To the extent they are true, then, these stories document a point seldom made: men with the power to affect women's careers allow sexual factors to make a difference. So the threats are serious: those who do not comply are disadvantaged in favor of those who do. (It is also seldom considered that a woman might be an attractive sexual object to her superior for the same reasons that *qualify* her for the position.)

Further, there may be compelling explanations for these stories other than their truth. How many men find it unbearable that a woman out-qualifies them in an even competition? Perhaps they assuage their egos by propagating rumors that the woman used her sexuality—something presumptively unavailable to men—to out-distance them. These stories may exemplify a well-documented inability of both sexes to see women in any but sexual terms. Willingness to believe the stories may illustrate the pervasive assumption that, since a career is so intrinsically inappropriate for a woman, her sexuality must define her role in this context, as well as in all others. This dovetails with the prior assumption that if a woman's sexuality is present at all, she must be receiving unfair consideration.

Certainly it is important to establish in individual cases whether a woman is complaining about a failed attempt cynically to use sex to get ahead or a bona fide situation of sex imposed as a career requirement. But to believe that instances raised in situation three symmetrically outweigh the injury that women as a whole suffer from sexual harassment ignores the evidence and provides a convenient excuse not to take the problem seriously. Whatever they mean, people who do not take sexual harassment seriously are an arm of the people who do it.

CONDITION OF WORK

In the quid pro quo, the coercion behind the advances is clarified by the reprisals that follow a refusal to comply. Less clear, and undoubtedly more pervasive, is the situation in which sexual harassment simply makes the work environment unbearable. Unwanted sexual advances, made simply because she has a woman's body, can be a daily part of a woman's work life. She may be constantly felt or pinched, visually undressed and stared at, surreptitiously kissed, commented upon, manipulated into being found alone, and generally taken advantage of at work—but never promised or denied anything explicitly connected with her job. These events occur both to "token women," whose visibility as women is pronounced and who often present a "challenge" to men,[55] and to women in traditional "women's jobs," who are defined as accessible to such incursions by the same standard that gives them the job at all. Never knowing if it will ever stop or if escalation is imminent, a woman can put up with it or leave. Most women hardly choose to be confronted by "the choice of putting up with being manhandled, or being out of work."[56] Most women are coerced into tolerance.

This feature of women's lives has sometimes surfaced in other people's lawsuits, although it has not been previously considered actionable in itself. One case from 1938 presents a zenith in women's vicarious relationship to the workplace. A long-time employee alleged (without success) that he was fired because his wife refused his superior's sexual advances.[57] In another case for reinstatement and back pay, in which the employer was accused of firing an employee because of his union activity, one comes upon the following account of the employee's conduct on the job:

He regularly made lewd remarks and suggestions to the waitresses and customers. . . . He caused at least one waitress to quit her job when he told her she would have to have sexual relations with him or he would make life difficult for her. He made similar advances to another waitress. Once Nichols called a waitress over to where he was seated drinking with a customer and solicited her to engage in an act of prostitution with the customer.[58]

Sexual harassment is effective largely because women's employment status is depressed. The following account, a composite of several individual accounts, illustrates the interplay of women's feelings of inadequacy with an objective assessment of their options in the labor market. The employer has an eye for energetic, competent, chronically underemployed women in a captive labor market (such as spouses of university men). They are intimidated by the work world. For the first time in their lives, the job gives these women responsibilities, a real salary, a chance to be creative, and quick advancement for good performance. They are grateful; "thrilled." They love the work and feel recognized for their achievements and potential. They work hard and create a niche for themselves. They need the money. Then, beginning on off-times, perhaps when there are unusual work demands, the underlying sexual innuendo is made explicit. Or the man sends the woman on a business trip, shows up at the hotel room where he had booked her, and rapes her.

At this point, otherwise small things come together: all the other women who have precipitously left "such a good job"; the number of women on long, paid leaves that become terminal; the stereotypically attractive appearance of the women, including a ban on long pants at the office. To an individual woman, his demand that she be constantly emotionally available to him; increasingly using her "as a verbal carpet"; his jealousy of her friendships on the job; his casual, even concerned inquiry into her sex life; his lack of desire to meet her husband and his uncomfortableness (or transparent obsequiousness) when he drops in. It becomes clear that his personnel policy is based on his sexual feelings.

Given the woman's insecurity about her work competence, the job may begin to seem like make-work to her, an excuse to keep her available so long as she is sexually compliant, or he thinks she might be. Or the job may continue to be very important to her. Surely she knows there are many women just like her who will take her place if she leaves. Should a woman have to leave a job she needs financially, qualifies for, or finds fulfilling because the employer can make his sexual needs part of it? Or should she have no recourse other than the hope he will stop, or never try again, or that she can stand it just for the chance to work there, or to work at all? Will it ever be different any place else? When workplace access, advancement, and tolerability (not to mention congeniality) depend upon such an employer's good will, women walk very thin lines between preserving their own sanity and self-respect and often severe material hardship and dislocation.

Two recent cases of women seeking unemployment compensation from jobs they left because of employer sexual harassment illustrate the problem, with variations, in somewhat more detail. In a California case,* Nancy Fillhouer[59] left work because she could no longer tolerate the remarks of her employer, which were "slan-

---

* This case is discussed in detail in chapter 4, *Sexual Harassment,* at 80–81.

derous, crude and vulgar," and because he had "tried to exploit her, thus making her job unbearably difficult from an emotional standpoint." In the language of the referee:

She said he was constantly remarking concerning his wishes to have sexual contact with her, and that she reacted in such a way as to certainly inform him that such intentions were not welcome. When she would walk by him, he would occasionally pat her behind. He would make comments to his friends about her figure or legs whenever she wore a dress, implying that she was a loose woman and would do anything with anyone. The claimant asserted that the employer attempted to arrange a liaison with one of his friends for a price. On another occasion, she said one of his friends came to the office and made a comment about the weather being cold, and the employer said that the claimant could keep him warm.[60]

In a similar case in New York State, Carmita Wood[61] reported that she was forced to leave her job because of the physical and emotional repercussions of a superior's sexual advances. He constantly "incorporated palpably sexual gestures into his movements."[62] When speaking to her "he would lean against her, immobilizing her between his own body and the chair and the desk."[63] Sometimes he would "stand with his hands shaking in his pockets and rock against the back of a chair, as if he were stimulating his genitals."[64]

A similar barrage of indignities sustained by one woman in her job as a "photo finishing girl" at a camera store in Oregon† provides a third example. Her complaint alleges that on many occasions her superiors and co-workers, in the presence of other employees and customers, "peer[ed] down plaintiff's blouse from the upper level and stairways above the main sales area of Mr. Pix Camera Store, assisted by binoculars or telephoto lenses." In addition to making frank propositions and references to the large size of her breasts and of their penises, the defendants described the woman as desiring them sexually. Specific statements included:

† This case, *Fuller v. Williames,* No. A7703-04001 (Portland, Oregon), is discussed in chapter 6, *ibid.* at 168–69.

'Did you just have sex with your husband? What was it like?'; 'Is that all you do is have sex with your husband?'; 'Do you sleep naked with your husband, pointing out that women were 'better off in bed,' meant 'only for the bedroom or the kitchen,' that plaintiff and other women employees were 'only interested in sleeping with the male employees,' that the former photofinishing 'girl' 'was a good lay. We screwed her down in the basement. We all had sex with her.'; 'Do you think your husband would let me take his pants off in front of my camera if I lined him up with a nude female model?'; 'Tell your husband I want to do nudes of him. I must photograph him,' that plaintiff was unfit to perform her duties, that women, including plaintiff, were 'not fit for the photography business,' 'incompetent,' unable to work under pressure without bursting into tears,' 'couldn't take it,' 'often stayed home due to headaches,' 'can't be relied upon,' 'possess a lesser ability to photograph,' 'don't know which end of a camera is up,' 'get shows in galleries by sleeping with gallery directors,' 'We've never had a girl selling cameras here. It might be an interesting experiment.' 'We can't hire a woman who has a boyfriend or a husband and have them last any length of time because their partners become very jealous of all us good looking males.'[65]

The connections between sexual desirability and contempt for women, the denigration of women as workers, and exclusion of women from job opportunities have seldom been more vivid. All the careful admissions that women may be oversensitive cannot overwhelm the fact that such comments make women feel violated for good reason. Nor are these remarks aberrations. They make graphic and public the degradation women commonly experience as men's sexual playthings.

At no point in these cases was there an attempt to force the victim into more extensive sexual involvement. But the only reason sexual intercourse was not included was that the perpetrator did not so choose. Nor were the women told that if they did not submit to this molestation, they would be fired, although again this was the employer's choice. The victim's active cooperation with, or submission to, this behavior is relatively irrelevant to its occurrence. Short of physical assault, there is very little one can do to stop someone intent upon visual and verbal molestation, particularly if one has access to few forms of power in the relationship. These are hardly "arm's length" transactions, with the man as dependent upon an affirmative response as the woman is upon maintaining his good will. They are transactions which make his sexism a condition of her work.

Sexual harassment as a working condition often does not require a decisive yes or no to further involvement. The threat of loss of work explicit in the quid pro quo may be only implicit without being any less coercive. Since communicated resistance means that the woman ceases to fill the implicit job qualifications, women learn, with their socialization to perform wifelike tasks, ways to avoid the open refusals that anger men and produce repercussions. This requires "playing along," constant vigilance, skillful obsequiousness, and an ability to project the implication that there is a sexual dimension to, or sexual possibilities for, the relationship, while avoiding the explicit "how about it" that would force a refusal into the open.

A cocktail waitress, whose customer tips measure her success at this precarious game, reflects upon it.

[A waitress] must learn to be sexually inviting at the same time that she is unavailable. This of course means that men will take out their lust vicariously through lewd and insinuating words, subtle propositions, gestures. She must manage to turn him off gently without insulting him, without appearing insulted. Indeed she must appear charmed by it, find a way to say no which also flatters him.[66]

Another waitress makes the economic connection explicitly:

[Men think] they have a right to touch me, or proposition me because I'm a waitress. Why do women have to put up with this sort of thing anyway? You aren't in any position to say "get your crummy hands off me" because you need the tips. That's what a waitress job is all about.[67]

Still another corroborates:

Within my first month as a waitress, it was made very clear to me that if you are friendly enough, you could have a better station, better hours, better everything. . . . If you're tricky enough, you just dangle everybody but it reaches a point where it's too much of a hassle and you quit and take something else. But when you have children, and no support payments, you can't keep quitting.[68]

While these women's responses do not constitute "compliance" in the fullest sense, in another sense nonrejection is all the compliance that is required.

Noncompliance is very problematic when sexual harassment is a working condition. Consider the opportunities for rejection, both immediate and long term, allowed by the situation depicted in the following woman's statement, prepared in an attempt to organize the women in her office:

I, _____, do hereby testify that during the course of my employment with the [company] I have suffered repeated and persistent sexual harassment by Mr. X, [head] of the [company].

Mr. X has directly expressed prurient interest in me on several occasions when he called me into his office as an employee, in his capacity as my superior, during normal working hours. I have been made audience to sexually explicit language and imagery in Mr. X's office during normal working hours. I have been intimidated by his power over my job and future, his connections in [the local government], his reputation for vindictiveness, and the gun he carries, often visibly. In his office, Mr. X has initiated physical sexual contact with me which I did not want.

I believe, and have been made to feel by Mr. X, that my well-being on the job and advancement as an employee of the [company], as well as my recommendations for future jobs, are directly contingent upon my compliance with Mr. X's sexual demands.

It is my opinion that Mr. X's hiring procedures are directly influenced by his sexual interests and that most if not all women who work for the [company] undergo some form of sexual harassment.

Tolerance is the form of consent that sexual harassment as a working condition uniquely requires. The evidence of such cases after they *become* quid pro quo tends to confirm the implicit judgment by the woman who "goes along": it is important, beyond any anticipated delivery, to maintain the *appearance* of compliance with male sexual overtures, a posture of openness. In many cases, the men seem only to want to know they can have a date, to be able "accidentally" to touch a woman intimately at will, or, in a verbal analogue to exhibitionism, say sexy words in her presence, while acting as if something else entirely is happening. The telling aspect is that the decisively nontolerating woman must suddenly be eliminated. Her mere presence becomes offensive; to be reminded of her existence, unbearable. Desperate strategies are devised, including flat lies, distortions, and set-ups, to be rid of her immediately. Something fundamental to male identity feels involved in at least the appearance of female compliance, something that is deeply threatened by confrontation with a woman's real resistance, however subtly communicated. At the point of resistance the quid pro quo that was implicit all along in the working condition—the "tolerate it or leave" in her mind becomes "now that you don't tolerate it, you're leaving" from the boss—is forced into the open, and the two categories converge.

Before this point, the issues are considerably more difficult. The examples suggest that when sexual harassment occurs as a condition of work, it does not require compliance, exactly, on the woman's part. For consummation, nonrejection is not even required; rejection often has no effect. Since little or no active participation or cooperation is required of women in these sexual situations, how explicit should rejection have to be before she can protest the treatment? This is somewhat analogous to asking how ardently a woman must resist rape before she will be considered to have resisted, that is, not to have consented to it. In a case of sexual harassment, it would be paradoxical if, so long as a superior has the power to force sexual attentions by adopting forms of sexual expression that do not require compliance—for example, sitting naked in his office in her presence while giving dictation—a woman would be precluded from legal action or other complaint because she had not properly "refused." How is nontolerance to be conveyed? She can threaten or throw tantrums, but ultimately, what is she supposed to do besides leave work?

Should women be required to counterattack in order to force the man into explicit employment retaliation so she has something to complain about? The problem here is again analogous to a problem with the rape laws: a victim who resists is more likely to be killed, but unless she fights back, it is not rape, because she cannot prove coercion. With sexual harassment, rejection proves that the advance is unwanted but also is likely to call forth retaliation, thus forcing the victim to bring intensified injury upon herself in order to demonstrate that she is injured at all. Aside from the risks this poses to the woman, in a situation not her fault, to require a rejection amounts to saying that no series of sexual advances alone is sufficient to justify legal intervention until it is expressed in the quid pro quo form. In addition, it means that constant sexual molestation would not be injury enough to a woman or to her employment status until the employer retaliates against her *job* for a sexual refusal which she never had the chance to make short of leaving it. And this, in turn, means that so long as the sexual situation is constructed with enough coerciveness, subtlety, suddenness, or one-sidedness to negate the effectiveness of the woman's refusal, or so long as her refusals are simply ignored while her job is formally undisturbed, she is not considered to have been sexually harassed.

IMPACT OF SEXUAL HARASSMENT

Women's feelings about their experiences of sexual harassment are a significant part of its social impact. Like women who are raped, sexually harassed women feel humiliated, degraded, ashamed, embarrassed, and cheap, as well as angry. When asked whether the experience had any emotional or physical effect, 78 percent of the Working Women United Institute sample answered affirmatively. Here are some of their comments:

As I remember all the sexual abuse and negative work experiences I am left feeling sick and helpless and upset instead of angry. . . . Reinforced feelings of no control—sense of doom . . . I have difficulty dropping the emotion barrier I work behind when I come home from work. My husband turns into just another man. . . . Kept me in a constant state of emotional agitation and frustration; I drank a lot. . . . Soured the essential delight in the work. . . . Stomach ache, migraines, cried every night, no appetite.[69]*

* Ellipses separate different persons' responses.

In the Working Women United Institute study, 78 percent of the women reported feeling "angry," 48 percent "upset," 23 percent "frightened," 7 percent "indifferent," and an additional 27 percent mentioned feeling "alienated," "alone," "helpless," or other. They tend to feel the incident is their fault, that they must have done something, individually, to elicit or encourage the behavior, that it is "my problem."[70] Since they believe that no one else is subjected to it, they feel individually complicit as well as demeaned. Almost a quarter of the women in one survey reported feeling "guilty."

Judging from these responses, it does not seem as though women want to be sexually harassed at work. Nor do they, as a rule, find it flattering. As one explanation for women's apparent acquiescence, Sheila Rowbotham hypothesizes that (what amounts to) sexually harassed women are "subtly flattered that their sex is recognized. This makes them feel that they are not quite on the cash nexus, that they matter to their employer in the same way that they matter to men in their personal lives."[71] While the parallel to home life lends plausibility to this analysis, only 10 percent of the women in the Working Women United Institute sample and 15 percent of the *Redbook* sample* reported feeling "flattered" by being on the sex nexus. Women do connect the harasser with other men in their lives, but with quite different results: "It made me think that the only reason other men don't do the same thing is that they don't have the power to." The view that women really want unwanted sex is similar to the equally self-serving view that women want to be raped. As Lynn Wehrli analyzes this:

Since women seem to "go along" with sexual harassment, [the assumption is that] they must like it, and it is not really harassment at all. This constitutes little more than a simplistic denial of all we know about the ways in which socialization and economic dependence foster submissiveness and override free choice. . . . Those women who are able to speak out about sexual harassment use terms such as "humiliating," "intimidating," "frightening," "financially damaging," "embarrassing," "nerve-

* In both surveys, women could indicate as many feelings as they felt applied to them.

wracking," "awful," and "frustrating" to describe it. These words are hardly those used to describe a situation which one "likes."[72]

That women "go along" is partly a male perception and partly correct, a male-enforced reality. Women report being too intimidated to reject the advances unambivalently, regardless of how repulsed they feel. Women's most common response is to attempt to ignore the whole incident, letting the man's ego off the hook skillfully by *appearing* flattered in the hope he will be satisfied and stop. These responses may be interpreted as encouragement or even as provocation. One study found that 76 percent of ignored advances intensified.[73] Some women feel constrained to decline gently, but become frustrated when their subtle hints of lack of reciprocity are ignored. Even clear resistance is often interpreted as encouragement, which is frightening. As a matter of fact, any response or lack of response may be interpreted as encouragement. Ultimately women realize that they have their job only so long as they are pleasing to their male superior, so they try to be polite.[74]

Despite the feelings of guilt, self-loathing, and fear of others' responses, many women who have been sexually harassed do complain about it to someone—usually a woman friend, family member, or co-worker. About a quarter of them complain to the perpetrator himself.[75] Those who complain, as well as those who do not, express fears that their complaints will be ignored, will not be believed, that they instead will be blamed, that they will be considered "unprofessional," or "asking for it," or told that this problem is too petty or trivial for a grown woman to worry about, and that they are blowing it all out of proportion. Carmita Wood's immediate supervisor, to whom she had reported incidents with her other superior at length, when asked to recall if she mentioned them, stated: "I don't remember specifically, but it was my impression, it was mentioned among a lot of things that I considered trivia."[76]

Women also feel intimidated by possible repercussions of complaint, such as being considered a "troublemaker,"[77] or other men in their lives finding out about the incidents, men who typically believe they must have been asking for it. One article reports a man "recalling a woman purchasing clerk who had just received a 'really good raise' and then showed up at work 'all black and blue.' Her husband had 'slapped her around' because he thought the raise was a result of 'putting out.' "[78] Women students (and women junior faculty) fear the repercussions of complaint more than the academic and professional consequences of the harassment itself.[79]

Women's worst fears about the impact of complaint are amply justified. "Most male superiors treat it as a joke, at best it's not serious. . . . Even more frightening, the woman who speaks out against her tormentors runs the risk of suddenly being seen as a crazy, a weirdo, or even worse, a loose woman."[80] Company officials often laugh it off or consider the women now available to themselves as well. One factory worker reports: "I went to the personnel manager with a complaint that two men were propositioning me. He promised to take immediate action. When I got up to leave, he grabbed my breast and said, 'Be nice to me and I'll take care of you.'"[81]

Unions' response to women's complaints of sexual harassment by management has been mixed. Some union officials refuse to process grievances based upon claims of sexual harassment. In one such case,[82] the complainant sued the union for breach of its duty of fair representation. Ms. Gates, the company's first and only woman employee, was hired as a janitor on the day shift, then reassigned to the night shift.

While on the graveyard shift she was assigned to clean men's restrooms, to which she did not object except for the treatment which she allegedly received while doing her work. She complained that men were using the urinals while she was cleaning; that on occasions she was propositioned and chased around the restrooms, and that the company refused to place locks on the doors to prevent this from happening.[83]

Her doctor stated that the resulting emotional breakdown made her physically unable to work the night shift. The company then fired her on the grounds that she was unable to perform the work for medical reasons. Through its woman president, the union maintained that the firing was for good cause and urged Ms. Gates to accept the company's offer of reinstatement under the same

45

working conditions. When she refused, the union declined to process her claim, a decision the court held was for the union to make.*

Firm union support was given to four women in another shop who complained to the union of sexual harassment by a male foreman. The National Labor Relations Board reportedly "decided that the foreman would have to apologize to each woman and from then on our relationship would be strictly business."[84] The women found this inadequate. The union continued to pursue the issue, intervening directly in their relations with the perpetrator and working to change the pervasive attitude that "any woman who works in an auto plant is out for a quick make."[85] It should be noted that this assumption is not limited to auto plants. Men in almost every working context attribute sexual desire to women workers based upon their mere presence as workers in that particular environment. This assumption is professed equally about women who are seen as anomalies on the job (any woman who would seek a male-defined work situation must be there because of men) as for those who are in women's jobs (any woman who would choose a feminine job must be looking for a man). Since no working context is excluded, one cannot conclude that women select particular jobs for sexual reasons. As with rape, the situation seems more to be that men wish to believe that women desire to be sexually attacked and to that end construct virtually any situation as an invitation. Constructed according to these images, women who do convey any sexuality whatever are assumed to be unselective: "If you express any sexuality at all, they just assume you're available to them—you know, just anybody."

As a further result of such attitudes, complaining to the perpetrator usually has little good effect. The refusal is ignored or interpreted as the no that means yes. If the no is taken as no, the woman often becomes the target of disappointed expectations. She is accused of prudery, unnaturalness, victorianism: "What's the matter, aren't you liberated? I thought nothing bothered you." And lesbianism. The presumption seems to be that women are supposed to want sex with men, so that a woman who declines sexual

* This case is *Gates v. Brockway Glass Co., Inc.*, 93 L.R.R.M. 2367 (C.D. Cal. 1976). Sex discrimination was apparently not raised.

contact with this particular man must reject all sex, or at least all men. Noncooperative women (including women who carry resistance to the point of official complaint) are accused of trying to take away one of the few compensations for an otherwise meaningless, drab, and mechanized workplace existence, one of life's little joys.[86] This essentially justifies oppression on the basis of what it does for the oppressor. When the man is black and the woman white, the emotional blackmail, the "you're not the woman I took you for," often becomes particularly unfortunate. The American heritage of racism that portrayed the white woman as "too good" for the black man is now used to manipulate her white guilt, putting her in the position of seeming to participate in that system's castration of the black man if she declines to have sex with him, and in racist repression if she complains officially.

Women's confidence in their job performance is often totally shattered by these events. They are left wondering if the praise they received prior to the sexual incident was conditioned by the man's perception of the sexual potential in the relationship—or is it only that the later accusations of incompetence are conditioned by his perception of the lack of this possibility? Attempting to decline gracefully and preserve a facade of normalcy also has its costs: "We've all been so polite about it for so long to the point we are nauseated with ourselves."

Jokes are another form that the social control over women takes. Women who consider noncompliance dread the degradation of male humor. At Carmita Wood's hearing, when she was describing disabling pains in her neck and arm which vanished upon leaving the job, the referee said, "So you're saying, in effect, that [the professor] was a pain in the neck?" On being told the perpetrator's age, the referee remarked, "Young enough to be interested anyway."[87] As the brief for Ms. Wood put it, "Nowhere is the existence of a persistent sexual harassment . . . questioned, it is merely treated lightly."[88] Trivialization of sexual harassment has been a major means through which its invisibility has been enforced. Humor, which may reflect unconscious hostility, has been a major form of that trivialization. As Eleanor Zuckerman has noted, "Although it has become less acceptable openly to express prejudices against women, nevertheless, these feelings remain under the surface, often taking the form of humor, which makes the issues seem trivial and unimportant."[89]

Faced with the spectre of unemployment, discrimination in the job market, and a good possibility of repeated incidents elsewhere, women usually try to endure. But the costs of endurance can be very high, including physical as well as psychological damage:

The anxiety and strain, the tension and nervous exhaustion that accompany this kind of harassment take a terrific toll on women workers. Nervous tics of all kinds, aches and pains (which can be minor and irritating or can be devastatingly painful) often accompany the onset of sexual harassment. These pains and illnesses are the result of insoluble conflict, the inevitable backlash of the human body in response to intolerable stress which thousands of women must endure in order to survive.[90]

Without further investigation, the extent of the disruption of women's work lives and the pervasive impact upon their employment opportunities can only be imagined. One woman, after describing her own experiences with sexual harassment, concluded:

Many women face daily humiliation simply because they have female bodies. The one other female union member at my plant can avoid contact with everyone but a few men in her department because she stays at her work bench all day and eats in a small rest room at one end of her department.[91]

For many women, work, a necessity for survival, requires self-quarantine to avoid constant assault on sexual integrity. Many women try to transfer away from the individual man, even at financial sacrifice. But once a woman has been sexually harassed, her options are very limited:

If she objects, the chances are she will be harassed or get fired outright. If she submits, the chances are he'll get tired of her anyway. If she ignores it, she gets drawn into a cat-and-mouse game from which there is no exit except leaving the job.[92]

Women do find ways of fighting back short of, and beyond, leaving their jobs.[93] As has been noted, nonrejection coupled with noncompliance is a subtle but expensive form. One shuffles when one sees no alternative. Women have also begun to oppose sexual harassment in more direct, visible, and powerful ways. The striking fact that black women have brought a disproportionate number of the sexual harassment lawsuits to date points to some conditions that make resistance seem not only necessary but possible. Protest to the point of court action before a legal claim is known to be available requires a quality of inner resolve that is reckless and serene, a sense of "this I won't take" that is both desperate and principled. It also reflects an absolute lack of any other choice at a point at which others with equally few choices do nothing.

Black women's least advantaged position in the economy is consistent with their advanced position on the point of resistance. Of all women, they are most vulnerable to sexual harassment, both because of the image of black women as the most sexually accessible and because they are the most economically at risk. These conditions promote black women's resistance to sexual harassment and their identification of it for what it is. On the one hand, because they have the least to fall back on economically, black women have the most to lose by protest, which targets them as dissidents, hence undesirable workers. At the same time, since they are so totally insecure in the marketplace, they have the least stake in the system of sexual harassment as it is because they stand to lose everything by it. Since they cannot afford any economic risks, once they are subjected to even a threat of loss of means, they cannot afford *not* to risk everything to prevent it. In fact, they often must risk everything even to have a chance of getting by. Thus, since black women stand to lose the most from sexual harassment, by comparison they may see themselves as having the least to lose by a struggle against it. Compared with having one's children starving on welfare, for example, any battle for a wage of one's own with a chance of winning greater than zero looks attractive. In this respect, some black women have been able to grasp the essence of the situation, and with it the necessity of opposition, earlier and more firmly than other more advantaged women.

Other factors may contribute to black women's leadership on this issue. To the extent they are sensitive to the operation of racism on an individual level, they may be less mystified that the sexual attention they receive is "personal." Their heritage of systematic sexual harassment under slavery may make them less tolerant of this monetized form of the same thing. The stigmatization of all black women as prostitutes may sensitize them to the real commonality between sexual harassment and prostitution. Feeling closer to the brand of the harlot, black women may more decisively identify and reject the spectre of its reality, however packaged.

The instances of sexual harassment described present straightforward coercion: unwanted sex under the gun of a job or educational benefit. Courts can understand abuses in this form. It is important to remember that affirmatively desired instances of sexual relationships also exist which begin in the context of an employment or educational relationship. Although it is not always simple, courts regularly distinguish bona fide relationships from later attempts to read coercion back into them. Between the two, between the clear coercion and the clear mutuality, exists a murky area where power and caring converge. Here arise some of the most profound issues of sexual harassment, and those which courts are the least suited to resolve.

In education, the preceptive and initiating function of the teacher and the respect and openness of the student merge with the masculine role of sexual mastery and the feminine role of eager purity, especially where the life of the mind means everything. The same parallel between the relationship that one is supposed to be having and the conditions of sexual dominance and submission can be seen in the roles of secretary and boss. Rosabeth Kanter notes that the secretary comes to "feel for" the boss, "to care deeply about what happens to him and to do his feeling for him," giving the relationship a tone of emotional intensity.[94] Elsewhere, she sees that a large part of the secretary's job is to empathize with the boss's personal needs; she also observes that, since the secretary is part of the boss's private retinue, what happens to him determines what happens to her. Kanter does not consider that there may be a connection between the secretary's objective conditions and her feelings—sexual feelings included—about her boss.

Although the woman may, in fact, be and feel coerced in the sexual involvement in some instances of sexual harassment, she may not be entirely without regard for, or free from caring about, the perpetrator. Further investigation of what might be called "coerced caring," or, in the most complex cases, an "if this is sex, I must be in love" syndrome, is vital. It is becoming increasingly recognized that feelings of caring are not the only or even a direct cause of sexual desires in either sex.[95] In light of this, it cannot be assumed that if the woman cares about the man, the sex is not coerced. The difficulties of conceptualization and proof, however, are enormous. But since employed women are supposed to develop, and must demonstrate, regard for the man as a part of the job, and since women are taught to identify with men's feelings, men's evaluations of them, and with their sexual attractiveness to men, as a major component of their *own* identities and sense of worth,[96] it is often unclear and shifting whether the coercion or the caring is the weightier factor, or which "causes" which.

This is not the point at which the legal cause of action for sexual harassment unravels, but the point at which the less good legal case can be scrutinized for its social truths. The more general relationship in women between objective lack of choices and real feelings of love for men can be explored in this context. Plainly, the wooden dichotomy between "real love," which is supposed to be a matter of free choice, and coercion, which implies some form of the gun at the head, is revealed as inadequate to explain the social construction of women's sexuality and the conditions of its expression, including the economic ones. The initial attempts to establish sexual harassment as a cause of action should focus upon the clear cases, which exist in profusion. But the implications the less clear cases have for the tension between women's economic precariousness and dependency—which exists in the family as well as on the job—and the possibilities for freely chosen intimacy between unequals remain.

There is a unity in these apparently, and on the legal level actually, different cases. Taken as one, the sexual harassment of working women presents a closed system of social predation in which powerlessness builds powerlessness. Feelings are a material reality of it. Working women are defined, and survive by defining themselves, as sexually accessible and economically exploitable. Because they are economically vulnerable, they are sexually exposed; because they must be sexually accessible, they are always economically at risk. In this perspective, sexual harassment is less "epidemic" than endemic.

Notes

1. Claire Safran, *Redbook Magazine* (November 1976), at 149 (hereinafter, *Redbook*). That respondents were self-selected is this study's most serious drawback. Its questions are perceptively designed to elicit impressionistic data. (The questionnaire was published in the January 1976 issue.) When the results are interpreted with these characteristics in mind, the study is highly valuable. Scholars who look down upon such popular journalistic forays into policy research (especially by "women's magazines") should ask themselves why *Redbook* noticed sexual harassment before they did.

2. Much of the information in this chapter is based upon discussions with ten women who shared their experiences of sexual harassment with me from five to twenty or more hours apiece. In addition, I have studied lengthy first person written accounts by five other women. Several women reported the situations and feelings of other women who were being sexually harassed by the same man they were discussing with me. Where permission has been sought and obtained, some of this material will be quoted or referenced throughout. Where quotations in this chapter are unattributed, or statements of fact (such as the racial characteristics of victims and perpetrators) or feelings (such as caring about the man involved) are not otherwise footnoted, they are derived from one or several women from my own research.

Finally, although the context was education rather than employment, much of my grasp of sexual harassment as an experience is owed to the extensive investigation conducted at Yale from 1976 to 1978 by the plaintiffs and the Yale Undergraduate Women's Caucus Grievance Committee in connection with *Alexander v. Yale,* 459 F. Supp. 1 (D. Conn. 1977). In this research, incidents involving at least half a dozen faculty members or administrators and a total of about fifty women were systematically uncovered and pursued, to the extent the victims were willing.

3. Sex on the job has not gone entirely unnoticed; it is only sexual harassment conceived as such that has been ignored. Two examples illustrate. One study entitled "Rape at Work" reports rapes of women on their jobs by hospital or prison inmates, students or clients; employers, superiors, or co-workers are not

mentioned. Carroll M. Brodsky, "Rape at Work," in Marcia J. Walker and Stanley L. Brodsky, eds., *Sexual Assault, the Victim and the Rapist* (Lexington, Mass.: D. C. Heath & Company, 1976), at 35–52. This study is useful, however, for observing dynamics of on-the-job rape that are also true for sexual harassment, whether it includes rape or not. Rape at work was experienced as worse than at other places because work had been seen as a safe place, where the woman did not have to be constantly on guard (at 43–44). And the site of the assault is difficult to avoid (at 44). In another study of "occupations and sex," the examination is divided between jobs "where the occupation involves sex"—cab driving, vice squad duty, and gynecology—and jobs "where the occupation is sex"—stripteasing and prostitution. James M. Henslin, *Studies in the Sociology of Sex* (New York: Appleton-Century-Crofts, 1971). This defines as the universe for study the rarified extremes of the convergence of sexuality with work to the neglect of the common experience of thousands of women. See, however, Carroll M. Brodsky, *The Harassed Worker* (Lexington, Mass.: Heath, 1976), at 27–28 for a useful if brief discussion.

4. Recent attempts to understand women's experience from women's point of view have produced upheavals in standard conceptions in many academic disciplines. One clear example is in the field of history. See Gerda Lerner, *The Female Experience: An American Documentary* (Indianapolis: Bobbs-Merrill, 1977), especially the introduction; Joan Kelly-Gadol, "The Social Relation of the Sexes: Methodological Implications of Women's History," *Signs: Journal of Women in Culture and Society,* vol. 1, no. 4 (1976), at 809–824; Hilda Smith, "Feminism and the Methodology of Women's History," in Berenice A. Carroll, ed., *Liberating Women's History* (Chicago: University of Illinois Press, 1976), at 369–384.

5. References to this survey come from three sources. One is my own interpretation of a simple collation of the marginals from the survey, generously provided by Working Women United Institute (hereinafter, WWUI). The total is 145 women, because 5 women both attended the speak-out and worked in Binghamton. Whenever possible, I will refer to the published article which reports some of the data and provides some analysis. Dierdre Silverman, "Sexual Harassment: Working Women's Dilemma," *Quest: A Feminist Quarterly,* vol. III, no. 3 (1976–1977), at 15–24 (hereinafter, Silverman). Finally, Lin Farley's testimony before the Commission on Human Rights of the City of New York, Hearings on Women in Blue-Collar, Service and Clerical Occupations, "Special Disadvantages of Women in Male-Dominated Work Settings" (April 21, 1975) (mimeograph) refers to the same study.

6. United Nations Ad Hoc Group on Equal Rights for Women, Report on the Questionnaire xxxvi, Report on file at the New York University Law Review, reported in Note, 51 *New York U. L. Rev.* 148, 149, n. 6.

7. Letter of December 8, 1976, from Marie Shear, public information officer of the division, to Lynn Wehrli, copy in author's file.

8. *Redbook,* at 217, 219.

9. Nancy Seifer, "Absent from the Majority: Working Class Women in America" (New York: Institute of Human Relations, National Project on Ethnic America of the American Jewish Committee, 1973), at 11.

10. *1975 Handbook,* at 28.

11. *Redbook,* at 217. The only study I have found that sheds further light upon the statistical prevalence of sexual harassment of women is Diana E. H. Russell's 1978 pretest interviews of ninety-two women randomly selected from San Francisco households. The general purpose of the study was to investigate sexual assault and rape. Her question #46a was: "Some people have experienced unwanted sexual advances by someone who had authority over them such as a doctor, teacher, employer, minister, or therapist. Did you ever have any kind of unwanted sexual experience with someone who had authority over you?" Responses to this question were 16.9 percent yes, 83.1 percent no. From an examination of the rest of the marginals, it seems possible that these results are low. The more specific and detailed the questions became, the higher the affirmative responses tended to be. A woman who was sexually harassed by more than one authority figure would be counted only once. The percentage of affirmative responses to this question is about the same as to the question about sexual experiences with close relatives, but lower than to those about rape. Several questions were asked about rape. Perhaps more questions on authority figures would have increased the prevalence figures. Since the sampling was done by households, the incidence of sexual harassment might not be as high as it would be in subsamples, for instance, of employed women only. Nevertheless, nearly one-fifth of *all women* is a lot of women. The most startling result of the pretest is that 34 respondents reported a total of 65 incidents of rape and attempted rape in the course of their lives, with a pair or group assault counted as one attack. This means that approximately one-third of all women have been raped, or experienced an attempted rape. The preliminary analysis of the full sample of 935 interviews was available April 1, 1979. Information from Diana F. H. Russell, "The Prevalence of Rape and Sexual Assault," *Summary Progress Report,* March 31, 1978; Appendix IV: Edited Interview Schedule with Marginals. This research was sponsored by the National Institute of Mental Health and funded through the Center for the Prevention and Control of Rape.

12. *Redbook,* at 217; Silverman, at 18.

13. Working Women United Institute (at 593 Park Ave., New York, N.Y. 10021) seems to have been the first to use these words as anything approaching a term of art, at first in connection with the case of Carmita Wood in October, 1975 (see note 61). The concept was also used and developed by the Alliance Against Sexual Coercion (P.O. Box-1, Cambridge, Mass. 02139), for example in their "Position Paper #1" (September 1976) and appears in Carroll Brodsky, *The Harassed Worker* (Lexington, Mass.: Heath, 1976), at 27–28.

14. Sheila Rowbotham, *Woman's Consciousness, Man's World* (London: Penguin, 1973), at 29–30.

15. Adrienne Rich, *The Dream of a Common Language, Poems 1974–1977* (New York: W. W. Norton & Co., 1978), "Cartographies of Silence," at 17.

16. This statement is supported by every study to date and by my own research. These dimensions of sexual harassment were further documented at a speak-out by Women Office Workers, 600 Lexington Avenue, New York, N. Y., in October 1975. Accounts of the event, and WOW's complaint to the Human Rights Commission, can be found in *Majority Report,* November 1–15, 1975; Paula Bernstein, "Sexual Harassment on the Job," *Harper's Bazaar* (August 1976); *New York Daily News,* April 22, 1976; *New York Post,* April 22, 1976.

17. WWUI.

18. Silverman, at 18.

19. The information from the *Redbook* study in this paragraph is at 217, 149.

20. WWUI.

21. *Redbook,* at 217.

22. The use of pornographic videotapes is reported in "2 Phone Executives Called Promiscuous—Witnesses Tell of Sex in Offices as Trial on Wrongful Death Nears End in Texas," *New York Times,* September 3, 1977. The legal action is for the wrongful death of the man who committed suicide on being accused of a fact pattern seeming to amount to sexual harassment of many women employees.

23. *Redbook,* at 149.

24. Silverman, at 18; *Redbook,* at 217, 219.

25. WWUI; in May 1974, the median weekly earning for women working full time was $124.00. *1975 Handbook,* at 126.

26. The quotations are Ms. Munford's allegations from the Joint Pre-Trial Statement in her case, at 7 and 8, respectively. The decision in the case is *Munford v. James T. Barnes & Co.,* 441 F. Supp. 459 (E.D. Mich. 1977). In addition to Munford, the plaintiffs in *Alexander* (Price), *Barnes,* and *Miller* (see chap. 1, *supra,* note 5) are black women charging sexual harassment by white men. (Diane Williams is a black woman charging sexual harassment by a black man.)

27. First Amended Complaint for Outrageous Conduct and Slander; Law Action for Unpaid Wages; Demand for Jury Trial, Count IX, *Fuller v. Williames,* No. A7703-04001 (Ore. Cir. Ct. 1977).

28. See the discussion of vertical stratification in chap. 2, MacKinnon, *Sexual Harassment.*

29. See the discussion of sex roles and sexuality, in chap. 5, *ibid.*

30. Working Women United Institute, "Speak-Out on Sexual Harassment," Ithaca, N. Y., May 4, 1975 (typescript), at 15.

31. *Id.,* at 30.

32. Peggy A. Jackson, quoted in Jane Seaberry, "They Don't Swing to Sex on the Beat," *Washington Post,* October 13, 1975.

33. *Monge v. Beebe Rubber,* 316 A.2d 549, 560 (N.H. 1974).

34. *Redbook,* at 149.

35. See discussion in chap. 6, *Sexual Harassment,* beginning p. 167. The reference is to the classic formulation by Herbert Magruder of the position that a

man should d]not be liable in tort for emotional harm resulting from his sexual advances. Magruder, "Mental and Emotional Disturbance in the Law of Torts," 49 *Harv. L. Rev.* 1033, 1055 (1936).

36. *Tomkins v. Public Service Electric & Gas Co.*, 442 F. Supp. 553 (D.N.J. 1976), *rev'd*, 568 F.2d 1044 (3d Cir. 1977).

37. Transcript of administrative hearing 171, 174, *quoted in* Brief for Appellant at 18–20.

38. *Alexander v. Yale*, 459 F. Supp. 1 (D. Conn. 1977).

39. My own research and, for example: "her new supervisor asked her to lunch to discuss a promotion. Over the meal, in a nearby hotel, he said that he wanted to go to bed with her that afternoon and that it was the only way they could have a working relationship." Ann Crittenden, "Women Tell of Sexual Harassment," *New York Times,* October 25, 1977.

40. Leslie Phillips, "For women, sexual harassment is an occupational hazard," *Boston Globe,* September 9, 1977.

41. *Tomkins, supra,* note 36 illustrates these consequences.

42. *Monge v. Beebe Rubber*, 316 A.2d 549 (N.H. 1974).

43. *Barnes v. Train*, 13 FEP Cases 123 (D.D.C. 1974), *rev'd sub nom. Barnes v. Costle,* 561 F.2d 983 (D.C. Cir. 1977). On this motion the allegations of fact are provisionally considered as if they were true.

44. *Williams v. Saxbe,* 413 F. Supp. 654, 655–6 (D.D.C. 1976). Order denying motion to dismiss and motion for summary judgment by Judge Richey.

45. Clerk's Record, *quoted in* Brief for Appellant, at 39.

46. *Id.*, at 80.

47. *Elliott v. Emery Air Freight,* No. C-C-75–76, slip opinion, at 2 (W.D.N.C. June 21, 1977).

48. Investigative Report, No. 8, 1972, *quoted in* Brief of Appellee, at 4.

49. Quoted in Enid Nemy, New York Times News Service, *Newark Star-News,* August 24, 1975. This is identical to the fact pattern in *Munford v. James T. Barnes & Co.,* 441 F. Supp. 459 (E. D. Mich. 1977).

50. *Redbook,* at 217. A recent complaint filed in the Alaska federal district court alleged that the woman was rejected for the position of equal employment officer with a pipeline contractor because she refused sexual relations with the employer's senior management official. *Rinkel v. Associated Pipeline Contractors, Inc.,* 16 E.P.D. 1P#8331 (D. Alaska 1977). See also Kerri Weisel, "Title VII: Legal Protection Against Sexual Harassment," 53 *Washington Law Review* 123 (1977), at 124.

51. Constantina Safilios-Rothschild, *Women and Social Policy* (Englewood Cliffs: Prentice-Hall, 1974), at 66.

52. The legal import of this and other possible complications for sexual harassment as a cause of action is discussed in chap. 6, *Sexual Harassment.*

53. Rothschild, *supra,* note 51, at 66.

54. *Loc. cit.*

55. See Rosabeth M. Kanter, *Men and Women of the Corporation* (New York:

Basic Books, 1977), at 233–236. Gloria Steinem has suggested that "sexual harassment might be called the taming of the shrew syndrome." "Women Tell of Sexual Harassment," *New York Times,* October 25, 1977. This may be true for women who are perceived as powerful, but my investigations suggest that as many, if not more, women are sexually harassed whom the perpetrators perceive as powerless.

56. Brief for Appellants, at 17, *Corne v. Bausch & Lomb,* 562 F.2d 55 (9th Cir. 1977).

57. *Comerford v. International Harvester Co.,* 235 Ala. 376, 178 So. 894 (1938). Discharge in revenge for what was termed "the superior's failure to alienate the affections of the employee's wife" was held to impose no employer liability under a contract of employment. Here, the contract expressly provided that the employee would not be terminated as long as his services were satisfactory. The supervisor had reported that the plaintiff's services were unsatisfactory in revenge for the employee's wife's refusal of the supervisor's sexual advances. The discharge, although found malicious and improper and based on a false report of unsatisfactory performance, was held within the employer's right under the contract. This is not atypical of judicial interpretation of employment contracts.

58. *NLRB v. Apico Inns of California,* 512 F.2d 1171, 1173 (9th Cir. 1975).

59. *In re Nancy J. Fillhouer,* No. SJ-5963, California Unemployment Insurance Appeals Board (May 12, 1975) (Referee), *rev'd,* Appeals Board Decision No. 7505225 (July 2, 1975).

60. This and prior statement are contained in the statement by the referee of allegations of claimant, Decision of the Referee, at 1.

61. *In re Carmita Wood,* App. No. 207, 958, New York State Department of Labor, Unemployment Insurance Division Appeal Board (October 6, 1975).

62. Brief for Claimant-Appellant, at 1.

63. *Id.,* at 2; Affidavit of Carmita Wood, at 3.

64. Affidavit of Carmita Wood, at 3.

65. *Fuller v. Williames,* No. A7703-04001 (Ore. Cir. Ct. 1977).

66. Shulamith Firestone, "On the Job Oppression of Working Women: A Collection of Articles" (Boston: New England Free Press, n.d.).

67. An unnamed woman quoted in Nemy, *supra,* note 49.

68. *Id.* (This is a different woman from that quoted in the foregoing quotation.)

69. Silverman, at 18, 19.

70. *Redbook,* at 149; WWUI; *all* my own cases.

71. Rowbotham, *supra,* note 14, at 90.

72. Lynn Wehrli, "Sexual Harassment at the Workplace: A Feminist Analysis and Strategy for Social Change" (M.A. thesis, Massachusetts Institute of Technology, December 1976).

73. Silverman, at 19.

74. All my cases and all the studies comment upon a need to be polite during the incident, or to exit politely.

75. WWUI; Silverman, at 19.

76. Statement by [Mr. X], Lab. of Nuclear Studies, Transcript at 37, *In re Carmita Wood,* Case No. 75-92437, New York State Department of Labor, Unemployment Insurance Division (Referee).

77. *Redbook,* at 219; all my own cases mentioned this fear as substantial, even paralyzing.

78. Bill Korbel, quoted in Lin Farley, "Sexual harassment," *New York Sunday News,* August 15, 1976, at 12.

79. One Yale graduate student observed: "A student making a major complaint would expose herself in a way that's more harmful than harassment. The complaint could have a much more profound effect on your future and the focus of your education than the instance of harassment." Quoted by Alice Dembner, "A Case of Sex Discrimination," *Yale Graduate-Professional,* vol. 7, no. 14 (March 6, 1978), at 7. See also "Sexual Harassment: A Hidden Issue" (Project on the Status and Education of Women, Association of American Colleges, 1818 R. Street, N.W., Washington, D.C. 20009, June 1978), at 3; and Donna Benson, "The Sexualization of Student-Teacher Relationships" (unpublished paper: Berkeley, California, 1977).

80. Lin Farley, quoted by Enid Nemy, *supra,* note 49; see also Farley's testimony, *supra,* note 5.

81. *Redbook,* at 219.

82. *Gates v. Brockway Glass Co., Inc.,* 93 L.R.R.M. 2367 (C.D. Cal. 1976).

83. *Id.,* at 2367. See also the account by Morris Stone, "Backlash in the Workplace," *New York Times,* June 11, 1978, Business Section, p. 3.

84. Michele Noah, "Sexual Harassment on the Job," *Sister Courage* (Boston, May 1978), at 9.

85. *Loc. cit.*

86. Transcript, Permanent Commission on the Status of Women, Public Hearing, New Haven, Connecticut, January 22, 1975. A study of the role of sex in the life of the cab driver suggests a similar attitude. James M. Henslin, *Studies in the Sociology of Sex* (New York: Appleton-Century-Crofts, 1971).

87. Transcript of hearing, *In re Carmita Wood,* Case No. 75-92437, New York State Department of Labor, Unemployment Insurance Division, at 19, 37.

88. Brief for Claimant-Appellant, *In re Carmita Wood,* App. No. 207, 958, New York State Department of Labor, Unemployment Insurance Division Appeal Board (October 6, 1975), at 19.

89. Eleanor L. Zuckerman, "Masculinity and the Changing Woman," in Zuckerman, ed., *Women and Men: Roles, Attitudes and Power Relationships* (New York: Radcliffe Club of New York, ca. 1975), at 65.

90. Lin Farley, testimony, *supra,* note 5, at 6.

91. Transcript, Permanent Commission on the Status of Women, *supra,* note 86, at 5.

92. Lin Farley, testimony, *supra,* note 5, at 3.

93. One example is provided in a recent news article which reported a strike

by eight waitresses against sexual harassment by the management at a restaurant in Madison, Wisconsin: "Ellen Eberle, a waitress at Dos Banditos said that sexual harassment by the management was a constant problem. 'Pete says he never touches 'his girls' but it's not true. He's touched me a number of times and I didn't like it and I've told him so. It's perverted and it makes me sick. He's very blatant about it and he makes gross jokes.' "The strike was called after the owners and management refused to listen to the grievances; the waitresses went back to work after a settlement that they described as a "complete victory." *Off Our Backs,* vol. VIII, no. 5 (May 1978), at 10.

94. Kanter, *supra,* note 55, at 88.

95. See discussion at 156–58, *Sexual Harassment.*

96. For commentary on this point written by men, see Jack Litewka, "The Socialized Penis," and other articles in *For Men Against Sexism,* Jon Snodgrass, ed. (Albion, Cal.: Times Change Press, 1977), at 16–35.

Chapter 3

Questions and Answers:

INTRODUCTION

To help you understand the law more easily we have asked and answered questions concerning sexual harassment. The questions are divided into the following categories:

1) Sexual Harassment: What is it?
2) You and Sexual Harassment
3) The Employer
4) The Equal Employment Opportunity Commission
5) The Law and the Courts
6) Federal Employees
7) Educational Institutions

Some questions and answers may belong in more than one section. We therefore suggest you read all the questions and answers. In addition, the NOW Legal Resource Kit and the Equal Employment Opportunity Commission Guidelines provide more in-depth answers and analysis. If your question is still left unanswered, we suggest you contact your local EEOC office, which is listed in Chapter 6, or your local legal aid office. Because sexual harassment law is a growing area with frequent new developments and court decisions, we suggest you contact an attorney before filing an actual lawsuit.

SECTION 1: SEXUAL HARASSMENT, WHAT IS IT?

1. What is sexual harassment?

—The exact definition is imprecise. It varies from case to case. It depends on the nature and seriousness of the conduct and whether it is repetitive or not, but in all instances it must be sexual conduct of an unwelcome nature. In its guidelines the Equal Employment Opportunity Commission has defined sexual harassment as:

> Unwelcome sexual advances, requests for sexual favors, and other verbal or physical conduct of a sexual nature constitute sexual harassment when (1) submission to such conduct is made either explicitly or implicitly a term or condition of an individual's employment, (2) submission to, or rejection of such conduct by an individual is used as the basis for employment decisions affecting such individual, or (3) such conduct has the purpose or effect of unreasonably interfering with an individual's work performance or creating an intimidating, hostile, or offensive working environment.

2. Is sexual harassment illegal?

—Yes. It is a form of sexual discrimination in violation of Title VII of the 1964 Civil Rights Act, the Civil Rights Act of 1991, and Title IX of the 1972 Education Amendments. It may also violate state laws on sexual discrimination. This book focuses on sexual harassment under federal law.

3. Must the harassing conduct be unwanted?

—Yes. Voluntary sexual conduct is not unlawful sexual harassment.

4. Does all *unwanted* sexual behavior qualify as sexual harassment?

—Yes, although your legal remedy will depend on the nature and severity of the harassment.

5. Does sexual conduct become unlawful when unwelcome?

—Yes.

6. What is unwanted sexual conduct?

—Conduct not solicited or encouraged by the employee where the conduct is undesirable or offensive.

7. Is sexual harassment a form of discrimination?

—Yes.

8. Is harassment of men by women sexual discrimination?

—Yes.

9. Is harassment of men by men sexual discrimination?

—Yes.

10. Is harassment of women by women sexual discrimination?

—Yes.

11. Can an employee sexually harass an employer?
    —Yes, but this is rare and would not be covered under Title VII.

12. Is peer harassment sexual harassment?
    —Peer harassment is a form of sexual harassment. It is harassment by one's colleagues or fellow workers or fellow students. Under federal law you will only have a legal remedy if you are an employee or a student. Peer harassment by friends is not covered under Title VII.

13. Can sexual harassment occur outside the office?
    —Yes.

14. Can sexual harassment take place on a date?
    —Yes, if the parties share the same workplace.

15. Can one episode be sufficient to be deemed sexual harassment?
    —Yes.

16. Must sexual harassment involve sexual touching?
    —No. Conversation or sexually suggestive comments can constitute sexual harassment.

17. Must there be coercion in sexual harassment?
   —Yes, actual or implied.

18. What is coercion?
   —Coercion is the imposition of an unwelcome advance.

19. Can a voluntary sexual relationship be deemed sexual harassment?
   —Yes, if the court finds that the sexual advances were not welcome.

20. Are any of the following defined as sexual harassment?
   a) unwanted sexual attention
   b) sexually suggestive comments
   c) threat of punishment for refusal to comply with sexual advances
   d) implying that sexual favors may lead to a raise or better grades?
   —Yes, they are all forms of sexual harassment.

SECTION 2: YOU AND SEXUAL HARASSMENT

1. What percentage of American women will experience some form of sexual harassment during their academic or working life?
   —50% to 88% of women.

2. Do most victims of sexual harassment come forward?
   —No. It is estimated that more than 90% of victims of sexual

harassment do not come forward or register a complaint for fear of loss of privacy and/or retribution.

3. Do sexually harassed victims who report the incident generally do so immediately?
   —No.

4. Is it important to file sexual harassment complaints promptly?
   —Yes, because the events are usually fresher in the victim's mind, and under federal and state law you must file your complaint within a certain time.

5. What can I do if I have been sexually harassed?
   a) Advise the harasser that the attention is unwanted.
   b) Keep a written record of
      1) what happened
      2) when it happened
      3) where it happened
      4) your response
      5) any witnesses
      6) who you told and what you said
   c) Try to find out if the harasser has harassed others.
   d) Report the harassment to your supervisor and ask the supervisor to see to it that the harassment is stopped.
   e) File a written complaint through the company's internal grievance system and/or through your university.
   f) If the harassment has not stopped you may also
      1) File a charge with the EEOC and/or
      2) File a lawsuit under Title VII
      3) File a lawsuit for tort where potential monetary damages are greater than a Title VII lawsuit, or under your state's law on sexual discrimination.

6. Should the person being sexually harassed ask the harasser to stop?

—Yes. You should state that the attention is unwelcome. By making the statement in writing, and keeping a copy for yourself, you are creating a record that will be helpful if the behavior continues.

7. Will it help to ask the harasser to stop?

—In the U.S. Merit Systems Protection Board survey, 61% stated that telling the person to stop made things better while 29% of the women said ignoring the harassment helped.

8. Should victims of sexual harassment consult with an attorney before proceeding with a formal complaint?

—It depends. Under federal law, if you work for a company with fifteen or more employees, or are a federal employee, you must file a complaint with the EEOC first. You can do this without an attorney. After the EEOC makes a decision you may want to consult with an attorney. If you work for a smaller company, you may need to contact an attorney to help you evaluate the relevant state laws and advise you of your likelihood of success.

9. What can you do if you can't afford a lawyer?

—First, contact your legal aid society or community legal service center. They may be able to help you find a low cost attorney with sliding fee schedules. You can also seek a lawyer who will represent you on a "contingency fee." The fee will then be paid *only* from your recovery.

10. Do male harassers often try to discredit the accuser?
    —Yes.

11. Are most sexual harassment cases actually settled out of court?
    —Yes.

12. Is confidentiality part of the settlement?
    —Generally, yes.

13. How long can a sexual harassment complaint take before it is resolved?
    —If there is no litigation it could take a year. If there is litigation, it will probably take longer.

14. Is there a typical sexual harasser?
    —No.

15. Is a sexual harasser likely to be a repeat harasser?
    —Yes.

16. Are there typical victims of sexual harassment?
    —No. People of all ages, races and backgrounds are subject to harassment.

SECTION 3: SEXUAL HARASSMENT AND THE EMPLOYER

1. Is sexual harassment prevalent in large companies?
—Yes. A recent survey by the American Management Association showed that 52% of its membership have dealt with allegations of sexual harassment within the past five years. In addition, many more cases go unreported.

2. Do large companies treat allegations of sexual harassment seriously?
—Usually. The same survey of the American Management Association indicated that only 19% of the cases were dismissed without action while 60% of the cases resulted in some form of disciplinary action.

3. Do most organizations have official policies on sexual harassment?
—Yes.

4. Should employers rely on EEOC anti-harassment guidelines in drafting their policy statements?
—Yes. See chapter 5.

5. What are some of the practical benefits of corporate preventative programs of sexual harassment?
a) Reduced possibility of harassment through education.
b) Publication of grievance procedures should lead to prompt corrective action.

c) Reduced anger generated and time lost in the resolution of such claims.

d) Reduced likelihood of problems resulting in lawsuits.

6. What procedures should enlightened companies have on sexual harassment?

a) A written, easily accessible policy statement.

b) Prompt and fair procedures for investigating complaints.

c) Prompt and fair procedures for resolving disputes.

d) A training program for supervisors and all employees.

7. Should companies publish their policy on sexual harassment?

—Yes. One model policy starts as follows:

"It is our company's policy to prohibit sexual harassment of one employee by another employee, supervisor or even customers. The purpose of this policy is not to regulate our employee's personal morality. Rather, it is to insure that, in the workplace, no one may harass another individual."

In addition, the execution of such a policy helps the company maintain that it never condoned misconduct.

8. Should an employer's internal grievance program provide confidentiality to the victim?

—Yes, for as long as possible. But you should check to see if your employer's policy does provide confidentiality.

9. Do companies prefer to resolve complaints before any lawsuit is filed?

—Yes.

10. In the face of sexual harassment are employers likely to take corrective action?
   —Yes.

11. Once a case of sexual harassment is filed, what are the options of the company?
   —The company may seek to settle or fight the charges of harassment.

12. What are the crucial ingredients of an internal complaint procedure?
   a) Confidentiality
   b) Accuracy
   c) Promptness
   d) Thoroughness
   e) Fairness

13. Should employees follow the internal grievance procedure of the employer?
   —Yes. Justice Thurgood Marshall in *Vinson,* the first Supreme Court case to deal with sexual harassment as a form of sex discrimination, stated, "Where a complainant, without any good reason, bypassed an internal complaint procedure she knew to be effective, a court may be reluctant to find constructive termination."

14. Can an employee file an EEOC charge before utilizing the employer's internal complaint or grievance procedure?
   —Yes.

15. Should employers always take prompt remedial action upon learning of evidence of sexual harassment?
—Yes.

16. Is the employer likely to investigate complaints of sexual harassment?
—Yes. An employer who fails to investigate a claim is more likely to be found liable.

17. What is the extent of the employer's duty to investigate?
—At a minimum the employer should conduct an investigation which includes interviews of the complainant and the alleged harasser. Potential witnesses should also be interviewed if they are available.

18. Should the employer take immediate action on receipt of a complaint?
—Yes.

19. What is the nature of such action?
—The employer should take whatever action is needed to stop the harassment.

20. Should the complaining employee cooperate with any investigation of sexual harassment?
—Yes.

21. Is the employer under an obligation to conduct a fair and impartial investigation?
—Yes.

22. Will employers be informed if a sexual harassment complaint is filed against them?
—Yes. The EEOC notifies employers of complaints within 10 days. If an employee files a lawsuit under state law then the employer must also be served with the complaint.

23. If an employee resigns may she/he state a case of sexual discrimination?
—Yes. If an employee is sexually harassed and the employer does not correct the situation, the employee may claim she/he was constructively discharged.

24. If you are not satisfied with the results of your company's investigation of your sexual harassment claim, what choices do you have?
—Make a complaint to the EEOC or file a lawsuit based on state law.

25. Is retaliation for filing complaints illegal?
—Yes. Employers are prohibited from discharging or discriminating against any employee or applicant for employment because he or she has made a complaint, assisted with an investigation, or instituted proceedings.

26. May an employer limit its liability for sexual harassment claims by introducing procedures and policies against sexual harassment and by instituting a grievance procedure?
     —Yes.

27. Are there different standards of liability for the employer in quid pro quo cases than hostile environment cases?
     —Yes. In quid pro quo cases the courts generally apply strict liability to the employer. In hostile environment cases the courts look to whether the employer knew or should have known about the hostile work environment.

28. Can employers be liable for sexual harassment of a co-worker who is not a superior?
     —Yes. If the employer knew or should have known and did not correct the problem.

29. Can an employer be liable for sexual harassment of its employees by non-employees?
     —Yes, if the employer knew of the harassment and failed to correct the situation.

30. Are employees more likely to be held liable if the harasser is a supervisor and not a co-worker?
     —Yes.

31. Are employers *always* liable for the harassment of their employees?

—No.

32. Can an employer reduce its vulnerability to claims of sexual harassment?

—Yes.

33. What can the employer do to reduce its vulnerability?

a) Publish a statement against sexual harassment.

b) Provide a program of education on gender issues to supervisors and employees.

c) Provide a formal and fair complaint procedure.

d) Conduct a prompt and fair investigation

e) Act in accordance with the results of the investigation.

34. Can an employer be sued by a victim of sexual harassment and also be sued by the harasser?

—Yes. The harasser can allege wrongful discharge, defamation of character and financial damages.

35. When does an employer become liable for sexual harassment by one of its employees?

—When the employer has knowledge of the harassment or should have had knowledge of the harassment and does not act to end the harassment. In quid pro quo cases the employer will generally be held responsible regardless of its knowledge of the supervisor's acts.

SECTION 4: EEOC

1. With what federal agency do you file a complaint of sexual harassment?
    —The Equal Employment Opportunity Commission and state or local antidiscrimination offices.
    See Chapter 6 for EEOC addresses across the United States.

2. What is the EEOC?
    —It is the Equal Employment Opportunity Commission of the United States and it is charged with enforcement of anti-discrimination laws in the workplace and in schools. The courts also have jurisdiction over any such complaints.

3. What are the purposes of the Equal Employment Opportunity Commission?
    a) Enforcing the Law.
    b) Issuing guidelines to interpret Title VII.
    c) Investigating Claims.

4. What are the EEOC guidelines?
    —In 1988 the EEOC issued guidelines on issues of sexual harassment. These guidelines are included in Chapter 5.

5. Are you required to go to the EEOC?
    —Under federal law, if your company has fifteen or more employees, you must go to the EEOC and file a complaint before you can file a federal lawsuit. If you work for a smaller

company, and if your state has laws against sex discrimination, you may be able to file a lawsuit without going to the EEOC.

6. Do EEOC Guidelines have the force of law?

—No. The guidelines, rules and regulations issued by the EEOC are considered by the courts, but need not be followed.

—In the Meritor case the Supreme Court stated that the EEOC guidelines "while not controlling upon the courts by reason of their authority, do constitute a body of experience and informed judgement to which courts and litigants may properly resort for guidance."

7. What is the difference between Section 2 of the EEOC Guidelines and Section 3 of the EEOC Guidelines?

—Section 2 applies to quid pro quo cases where sex is traded for work or benefits.

—Section 3 cases apply to a hostile environment where offensive sexual behavior is present but not related to financial rewards.

8. May anyone file a complaint with the EEOC?

—Yes. If your company has at least fifteen employees, then you must file a complaint with the EEOC before you can file a lawsuit in federal court for sex discrimination.

9. If my company employs only ten people, may I file a complaint with the EEOC?

—No. Title VII coverage is limited to employers with fifteen employees or more. You may, however, initiate a lawsuit in state courts if your state has sex discrimination laws or if other legal theories might entitle you to recover.

10. How long do I have to file my complaint with the EEOC?
—You must do so within 180 days of the harassment or within 300 days if you have previously filed with a state agency.

11. Do you need a lawyer to file a charge with the EEOC?
—No.

12. If you file a complaint with the EEOC will your employer be notified?
—Yes. The EEOC will notify your employer within ten days of your filing the complaint.

13. What does the EEOC then do?
—The EEOC then investigates and decides whether it will sue on behalf of the individual.

14. Will the EEOC investigate every complaint?
—Yes.

15. How long does the EEOC have to investigate?
—The EEOC has 180 days to investigate and decide whether it wishes to sue on behalf of the individual. If it doesn't sue, the complainant has 90 days to file a lawsuit. However, vari-

ous tort claims allow a filing from one to three years afterwards.

16. What will be the result of an EEOC investigation?
—The EEOC will either issue a finding of reasonable cause or no reasonable cause of discrimination.

17. If EEOC issues a finding of reasonable cause of discrimination what will the EEOC do next?
—First, the EEOC will attempt to resolve the dispute between you and the employer. Second, if informal settlement is not possible, the EEOC may bring a lawsuit against your employer. If this suit is not brought within six months from the filing of your complaint, you receive a "right to sue" letter. You will have 90 days after receipt of this letter to file suit.

18. How often does the EEOC elect to sue on behalf of the individual?
—In 1990 the EEOC filed suit in only 50 cases of 5,694 sexual harassment complaints.

19. If the EEOC finds no reasonable cause and does not file suit, what can the claimant do?
—The claimant may then find a lawyer to initiate a private suit.

20. Is there any advantage to filing a complaint in state court as opposed to filing a complaint with the EEOC?

—Yes. If the complaint indicates intentional infliction of emotional damage or wrongful discharge the complainant may be entitled to greater damages.

21. Can investigations be made without complaints?
    —No. EEOC can conduct investigations *only* if charges have been filed.

22. Are the names of complainants kept confidential?
    —The complainant's name is divulged to the employer when an investigation is made. Charges, however, are not made public by EEOC, nor can any of its efforts during the conciliation process be made public by EEOC or its employees. The aggrieved party, however, and the respondent are not bound by the confidentiality requirement. If court action becomes necessary, the identity of the parties becomes a matter of public record.

23. What does it mean if the EEOC issues a right to sue letter?
    —It means that the EEOC will *not* bring a case on your behalf. The letter will state whether the EEOC believes sexual harassment took place.

24. If the right to sue letter states that the EEOC does not believe sexual harassment took place, may I still sue?
    —Yes.

25. How soon after receiving a right to sue letter must I sue in federal court?

—The suit must be filed in 90 days.

26. Is there a fee for filing a claim with the EEOC?

—No.

27. If the EEOC decides to bring a sexual harassment case on your behalf do you have to pay them?

—No.

28. Will the EEOC ever expand an individual case to a "class claim"?

—Yes.

SECTION 5: THE LAW

1. What laws govern sexual harassment cases?

—Title VII of the Civil Rights Act of 1964 (amended in 1991) provides a basis for federal court action for employees in companies with 15 or more employees. You can only go to federal court after you file a complaint with the EEOC and wait for a decision. You may also sue in state court under state law if your state has laws against sexual discrimination or sexual harassment.

2. When was the phrase "sexual harassment" coined?

—1976.

3. When did the Supreme Court of the United States first recognize sexual harassment?
  —1986.

4. What is the significance of *Meritor Savings Bank v. Vinson*?
  —It is the first Supreme Court decision to define a hostile or threatening environment as a violation of Title VII and EEOC Guidelines and as sexual harassment.

5. What is Title IX of the Education Amendments of 1972?
  —It is a law that prohibits sex discrimination in educational institutions receiving federal funds.

6. Does suing for sexual harassment preclude a sexual discrimination claim under Title VII?
  —No.

7. Are Title VII claims decided by a judge or a jury?
  —They used to be considered by a judge but under the Civil Rights Act of 1991 any party to a case can demand a jury trial when compensatory or punitive damages are sought.

8. Can I get an injunction under Title VII?
  —Yes. An injunction is a decree which directs a party to cease and desist from prohibited actions.

9. Does Title VII protect you against discrimination based on sexual orientation?
    —No.

10. Does Title VII proscribe all sexual relationships in the workplace?
    —No. Welcome voluntary sexual relationships or sexual behavior is not prohibited by Title VII.

11. What forms of sexual harassment are recognized by the law?
    a) Quid pro quo cases
    b) Hostile environment cases

12. What is a quid pro quo case?
    —A case in which a teacher or supervisor demands sexual favors as a condition of good grades or employment.

13. Does a quid pro quo claim generally require a pattern of offensive conduct?
    —No. A single sexual advance related to granting or denying employment benefits can constitute sexual harassment. (For example, if the employer says "I won't give you a raise or promotion unless you sleep with me.")

14. What is a hostile environment case?
    —A case in which a teacher or supervisor permits an atmosphere where unwelcome sexual advances or unwelcome sexual innuendo occur.

—In 1991 a U.S. district judge in Florida ruled that the posting of soft and hardcore pornography and demeaning sexual remarks were forms of sexual harassment, because they constituted a hostile environment.

15. What other factors determine whether a work environment is hostile?
    —See Chapter 5.

16. What standards do the courts use for evaluating sexual harassment?
    —The harasser's conduct is evaluated from the point of view of the reasonable person.

17. Must hostile environment cases, according to the EEOC guidelines, be repeated or can a single incident qualify as a hostile environment?
    —Generally such incidents must be repeated and pervasive to qualify as a hostile environment.

18. Does a hostile environment claim generally require a pattern of offensive conduct?
    —Yes.

19. Are incidents of sexual harassment directed at other employees relevant in deciding whether there is a hostile work environment?
    —Yes.

20. Must the harassment be severe or perceived to be severe to be actionable?

—Yes. This was the position of the Supreme Court in the *Meritor* case.

21. Are acts of physical aggression, intimidation and hostility based on sex considered actionable sexual harassment?

—Yes.

22. Must the sexual harassment persist over a long period to be actionable?

—No.

23. Can a single episode qualify as sexual harassment?

—Yes, if the incident is blatant and severe.

24. Are sexual harassment claims limited to those in which a job benefit is withheld?

—No. In *Meritor Savings Bank v. Vinson,* the Supreme Court of the United States held that sexual harassment includes any offensive discriminatory work environment relating to sexual issues.

25. Are you a victim of sexual harassment if you are not harassed but are denied benefits in favor of those who participate in exchanging sexual relations for job benefits?

—Yes. This was decided by the U.S. Court of Appeals in Broderick v. Ruder which involved a hostile work environment at the Securities and Exchange Commission. Third parties can be injured by a sexual relationship between two other parties if they are denied job benefits.

26. Are there criminal laws against sexual harassment?
—Yes. Many states have laws related to sexual assault and/or sexual abuse.

27. What remedies to sexual harassment does the law provide?
—You can file a complaint with the Equal Employment Opportunity Commission or file a lawsuit in state court under your state's law. You may be entitled to compensation and damages. In one recent case in California the jury awarded almost one million dollars in damages against an employer for failing to take corrective action against a sexual harasser.

28. What other remedies are available to a victim of sexual harassment?
—If the employee was wrongfully discharged he or she could be reinstituted with back pay. If a promotion were wrongfully denied, the employee could receive the promotion and a retroactive pay increase. The employer may also be ordered to change its employment practices.

29. Are there state agencies to enforce sexual discrimination laws?
—Yes. Most states have such agencies.

30. Do states have equal employment laws that apply to sexual harassment?

—Most do.

31. Do cities have equal employment laws that apply to sexual harassment?

—Some do, but not all.

32. Do state workers' compensation laws apply to sexual harassment cases?

—Very often they do. A legal aid office or an attorney will be able to advise you on this.

33. Should I first file a complaint with the EEOC or the state agency?

—If your state has such an agency you must file a complaint with the state agency before filing a complaint with the EEOC, unless you work for the federal government or within the District of Columbia.

34. What should the complaint contain?

—Detailed evidence of the harassment as well as any actions taken to confront the harasser. All complaints should be in writing.

35. Should the complainant be prepared to substantiate his/her complaint?

—Yes. A complaint of sexual harassment generally elicits a

thorough investigation of all facts including interviews with the complainant and the harasser.

36. Should sexual harassment complaints be filed immediately?
—It is better to do so. You must file your complaint within certain time limits under state or federal law.

37. Should I gather corroborative evidence before instituting a sexual harassment claim?
—Yes.

38. Is it possible to sustain a claim of sexual harassment without corroborative evidence?
—It is possible but very difficult. Courts are much more likely to find that sexual harassment occurred if the victim has extensive corroboration.

39. Should there be third party corroboration of sexual harassment?
—It is generally much more difficult, but not impossible, to prove your case if there is no third party corroboration.

40. Who has the burden of proof in sexual harassment cases?
—The burden of proof belongs to the accuser.

41. If I bring a sexual harassment suit should I sue my employer?
—Yes. Under Title VII and case law the employer is generally responsible for damages for sexual harassment. This is particularly true in quid pro quo cases of harassment where benefits are granted or withheld by a supervisor in exchange for sexual favors. In "hostile environment" cases the employer is liable if it knew or should have known of the sexual harassment and did not correct the situation.

42. May a victim of sexual harassment also sue for a tort claim?
—Yes. A victim may be able to sue for assault and battery and emotional distress under the state's personal injury laws.

43. Under Title VII can you sue your co-worker for sexual harassment?
—No, but you can sue your employer and your supervisors for failing to stop sexual harassment.

44. Does Title VII provide for awards of attorney's fees and court costs to successful plaintiffs?
—Yes.

45. Can someone who believes she or he has been sexually harassed sue for monetary damages?
—Yes.

46. What is the effect of the 1991 Civil Rights Act on sexual harassment claims?

—The rights of the complainant were vastly expanded. You may now seek a financial award including both compensatory and punitive awards. However the 1991 Civil Rights Act did cap or put a ceiling on damages you can recover from your employer. The cap is:

Size of Company	Financial Cap
15–100 Employees	$50,000
101–200 Employees	$100,000
201–500 Employees	$200,000
Over 500 Employees	$300,000

In addition, the 1991 Civil Rights Act provided coverage to two additional groups of employees:

a) Overseas employees working for U.S. companies.

b) Employees of Congress.

47. Do juries ever render large awards in sexual harassment cases?

—Yes. While Title VII places a limit on some damages it may still be possible to recover additional damages under other legal theories. Recently the University of Iowa was ordered to pay a female professor over one million dollars. In California a jury awarded a law clerk almost $500,000 when her law firm did nothing to prevent her sexual harassment by her supervisor.

48. What legal theories would support claims of sexual harassment other than legislation?

—There are many such legal theories including assault and battery, intentional infliction of emotional distress, and invasion of privacy.

49. Are facts about a complainant's sexual history and off work conduct discoverable?
    —No.

50. Is the psychological history of a complainant discoverable?
    —Only where the complainant is seeking damages for emotional distress.

SECTION 6: FEDERAL EMPLOYEES

1. Is sexual harassment a problem in the federal government?
    —Yes. The U.S. Merit Systems Protection Board conducted a survey of sexual harassment in the Federal Government in 1988 and concluded that sexual harassment remains a widespread problem in the Federal workplace.

2. What were the main findings of the study?

Sexual Harassment In The Federal Government 1988

Executive Summary

This report discusses the results of a major 1987 survey and study dealing with sexual harassment in the federal workplace. It marks the second time the U.S. Merit Systems Protection Board has focused on this important topic. As an update, the report provides some contrasts and comparisons with data gathered in the Board's first landmark study of sexual harassment in 1980. It details findings on employee attitudes toward and experiences with uninvited behavior of a sexual nature. It also describes the actions federal agencies have taken in their efforts to reduce sexual harassment, and the financial as well as human costs when those efforts fall short. The report reviews relevant case law that has developed over the last 7 years as the Board and the courts have sought to define the legal rights and redress for victims of sexual harassment. It concludes with recommendations for future action within the government.

Background

In late 1979, the Subcommittee on Investigations of the U.S. House of Representatives' Committee on Post Office and Civil Service requested that the U.S. Merit Systems Protection Board (MSPB) conduct a thorough and authoritative study of sexual harassment in the federal workplace. The Board was asked to carry out the study since it is an independent, quasi-judicial agency that decides appeals from personnel actions taken against federal employees and conducts studies of the civil service and other merit systems. It is responsible for protecting the integrity of the federal civil service system from abuse.

The initial study of sexual harassment conducted by MSPB in 1980, with a final report issued in early 1981, was a "first of its kind" broad-scale survey of the attitudes and experiences of a representative cross section of both self-identified victims and nonvictims within the federal government.

In 1986, on its own initiative, the Board decided to conduct a followup study on sexual harassment to determine what changes, if any, had occurred in the federal government since the time of the first study. As part of this followup study, which was conducted in 1987, a questionnaire that replicated much of the original survey was used so responses for 1987 could be compared with the 1980 data. The questionnaire was sent to a representative cross section of approximately 13,000 federal employees, and 8,523 employees responded.

One of the difficulties inherent in any discussion of sexual harassment is that the term itself is a "term of art" that holds different meanings for different people. In late 1979, the U.S. Office of Personnel Management (OPM) issued a policy statement that defined sexual harassment as "deliberate or repeated unsolicited verbal comments, gestures, or physical contact of a sexual nature which are unwelcome." In 1980 the

Equal Employment Opportunity Commission (EEOC) issued guidelines on unlawful discrimination because of sex that expanded this definition. EEOC specified, for example, that conduct of a sexual nature could be considered sexual harassment if it created "an intimidating, hostile, or offensive working environment." The EEOC guidelines also noted that a determination of the legality of alleged sexually harassing conduct would be made from the facts, on a case-by-case basis.

Since the EEOC guidelines were issued, a body of legal precedents, including a 1986 Supreme Court decision, has provided legal clarification as to what constitutes sexual harassment. For purposes of this report, however, the Board relies upon the expressed views of federal employees for its definition. If a respondent to the Board's survey stated that he or she had received uninvited or unwanted sexual attention during the preceding 24 months, that was counted as an incident of sexual harassment even though not every incident, if fully investigated, would necessarily meet the legal definition of sexual harassment.

As this report discusses, sexual harassment in the workplace, like racial discrimination, can be a pervasive form of illegal discrimination that is both difficult to precisely measure and difficult to change. Yet, like racial discrimination, sexual harassment must be addressed so that positive change can occur. The purpose of this report is to clarify the nature and extent of the problem within the federal government, to review some of the actions taken during the last 7 years to address that problem, and to offer some suggestions for future efforts.

Summary of Findings

Compared to 7 years ago, federal workers are now more inclined to define certain types of behavior as sexual harassment. For example, in 1980 approximately 77 percent of all employees considered uninvited pressure for dates by a supervisor to be sexual harassment. In 1987 that percentage had increased to almost 84 percent. Likewise, in 1980, 84 percent of male employees and 91 percent of female employees considered unwanted supervisory pressure for sexual favors to be sexual harassment. In 1987 those percentages had increased to 95 percent and 99 percent, respectively. Similar changes were seen in employee attitudes about most other types of behavior.

In 1987, 42 percent of all women and 14 percent of all men reported they experienced some form of uninvited and unwanted sexual attention. Despite an apparent increase in the level of sensitivity about what behavior may be considered sexual harassment, there has been no significant change since the Board's last survey in 1980 in the percentage of federal employees who say they have received such uninvited and unwanted attention. Within the context of this report, unwanted and uninvited sexual attention is considered sexual harassment. Interestingly, among current federal employees who had also worked outside the federal government, the preponderant opinion is that sexual harassment is no more of a problem in the government than outside it.

The most frequently experienced type of uninvited sexual attention is "unwanted sexual teasing, jokes, remarks, or questions." The least frequently experienced type of harassment—"actual or attempted rape or assault"—is also arguably the most severe. Sexual harassment takes many forms and an employee may experience more than one form. In answering the Board's 1987 survey, 35 percent of all female respondents and 12 percent of all male respondents said they experienced some type of "unwanted sexual teasing, jokes, remarks, or questions." Also in 1987, approximately .8 percent of all female respondents and .3 percent of male respondents said they experienced "actual or attempted rape or assault."

The incidence rate for alleged sexual harassment varies by agency. For example, in 1987 a high of 52 percent of the female employees at the Department of State claimed they experienced some form of uninvited sexual attention, compared to a low of 29 percent of the female employees at the Department of Health and Human Services. Moreover, among the

16 agencies whose employees were surveyed in both 1980 and 1987, several did show some shifts in the percentage of employees claiming they experienced uninvited and unwanted sexual attention. A few agencies (for example, the Departments of Labor and Transportation) experienced a significant decline in the percentage of female employees who said they were harassed.

Co-workers are much more likely than supervisors to be the source of sexual harassment. In 1987, 69 percent of female victims and 77 percent of male victims said they were harassed by a co-worker or another employee without supervisory authority over them. Only 29 percent of the female victims and 19 percent of the male victims cited someone in their supervisory chain as the source of their harassment. This pattern is consistent with the Board's 1980 findings.

Some individuals are more likely than others to be victims of sexual harassment. For example, based on the data obtained in 1987, women who: are single or divorced; are between the ages of 20 and 44; have some college education; have a nontraditional job; or work in a predominantly male environment or for a male supervisor have the greatest chance of being sexually harassed. However, as the Board found in 1980, despite this generalization, sexual harassment is still widely distributed among women and men of all ages, backgrounds, and job categories.

Many victims tried more than one response to unwanted sexual attention. Although later judged ineffective by most of them, almost half of all victims tried to ignore the behavior or otherwise did nothing in response. In 1987, only 5 percent of both female and male victims said they took some type of formal action. Although most employees were aware of the availability of formal action—e.g., filing a grievance or a discrimination complaint—very few chose to use those potential remedies.

When victims of sexual harassment did take positive action in response to unwanted sexual attention, it was largely informal action and, in many cases, was judged to be effective. The most effective and frequently taken informal action was simply telling the harasser to stop. Forty-four percent of the female victims and 25 percent of the male victims said they took this action and, in over 60 percent of the cases, both groups said it "made things better."

Among the 22 largest federal departments and agencies surveyed, all had issued policy statements or other internal guidance during the 7-year period from FY 1980 through FY 1986 concerning prohibitions against sexual harassment. How frequently that guidance was updated and each agency's method of dissemination varied. Most employees, however, said they are aware of their agency's policies regarding sexual harassment and the internal complaint procedures available to victims.

Every agency maintained it provided training on the issue of sexual harassment, although most efforts were directed at managers and personnel and equal employment opportunity officials rather than nonsupervisory employees. Most (18 of 22) agencies estimated that during the 7-year period from FY 1980 through FY 1986, the average employee spent 2 hours or fewer in training related to sexual harassment. It should be noted, however, that agencies are not required to keep detailed records in this regard and, therefore, most responses tended to be "best estimates."

Most agencies maintained that they have taken a number of different actions in an effort to reduce sexual harassment and that, in most cases, those actions have been effective. Employees were more skeptical. For example, every agency surveyed said it provided "swift and thorough investigations of complaints" and that such investigations were effective. Only 32 percent of the employees surveyed felt their agencies provided such investigations.

During the two-year period from May 1985 through May 1987, sexual harassment cost the federal government an estimated $267 million.This cost is in addition to the personal cost and anguish many of the victims had to bear. This conservative estimate is derived by calculating the cost of replacing employees who leave their jobs as a result of sexual harassment, of paying sick leave to employees who miss work as a consequence, and of reduced individual and work group productivity.

Conclusions and Recommendations

Based on the findings discussed in this report, since the Board conducted its first study of sexual harassment, there is evidence that some positive changes have occurred in federal employee attitudes and perceptions regarding uninvited sexual attention. More employees, both men and women, are aware that certain behaviors of a sexual nature can be both unwanted and inappropriate in the workplace. In addition, most employees are now aware that sexual harassment is contrary to established agency policy. During this time, federal agencies have also taken a number of actions designed to reduce the incidence of sexual harassment and at least a few agencies have had some success in this regard.

Despite these positive trends, however, the overall bottom line did not change. Uninvited and unwanted sexual attention was experienced by almost the identical proportion of the work force in 1987 as in 1980. Sexual harassment is still a pervasive, costly, and systemic problem within the federal workplace.

The Board recommends that:

All agency employees should be periodically reminded of their responsibilities and held accountable for compliance with federal law and agency policy prohibiting sexual harassment in the workplace. It must be clear that sexually harassing behavior by any employee cannot and will not be tolerated. This can be accomplished in a number of ways, including issuing an agency policy statement signed by the head of the agency detailing the specific prohibited practices and the penalties associated with those practices. This statement should be updated annually or as needed. Agencies should also require each employee to acknowledge that he or she has read and understands the policy.

With regard to enforcement of the law and agency policies on sexual harassment, each agency should:

—Seek to identify, on its own initiative, possible instances of sexual harassment;

—Quickly and thoroughly investigate allegations (within 120 days if possible); and

—Establish and exercise strong sanctions against harassers where the facts warrant.

Federal agencies should provide training on sexual harassment to nonsupervisory employees as well as to managers and EEO and personnel officials. The training should include discussion of the various behaviors that may be construed as sexual harassment and, for victims, some of the appropriate and more effective responses possible. The training should also stress that individuals need to be sensitive to the ways in which their actions may be interpreted by others. Whether certain behavior constitutes sexual harassment depends not only on the intent behind the behavior but also on the perceptions of those affected.

Recommendations

Many times, there was an "old boys network" that served to tacitly condone or at least "look the other way" at cases of discrimination or harassment. This situation inhibits female employees from making complaints. The action I took to prevent sexual harass-

ment was to dress abnormally. That meant I either put on more clothes than normal, or dressed unattractively and out of style.
A Survey Respondent

Introduction
This report finds that sexual harassment remains widespread in the federal workplace. At the same time, agencies have established and publicized policies that prohibit sexual harassment on the job. Overall, Federal employees are aware of these policies. Agencies have also provided related training to their managers and personnel and EEO officials, as well as some of their nonsupervisors, so that they will understand what sexual harassment is and how to prevent it.

However, given the persistence and pervasiveness of sexual harassment in the Federal workplace, it is clear that efforts to prevent it have not been successful enough. Also, as the data indicate, many employees are skeptical about the efforts of their agencies to deal with the problem.

As this report has discussed, there is still considerable confusion and disagreement about what behaviors can constitute sexual harassment. Part of this disagreement may well stem from the fact that whether an action or behavior constitutes sexual harassment depends not only on the intent of the person taking the action but also on the perceptions of those affected by it. Based on the responses to the Merit Systems Protection Board's latest questionnaire, a considerable percentage of federal employees experience unwelcome and uninvited behavior of a sexual nature on the job. It is this behavior which this report defines as sexual harassment.

Based on the results of this study, it also appears that some managers and employees do not take the prohibition against sexual harassment seriously.

The courts are continuing to develop and refine case law on sexual harassment. In the process they are leveling penalties against the men and women they find responsible. Courts at various levels are repeatedly supporting the EEOC guidelines on sexual harassment as a violation of Title VII of the Civil Rights Act of 1964. Aggressive action to ensure that the federal workplace is free from sexual harassment is both proper and in the best interests of the government. To assist federal agencies in this regard, we recommend the following actions.

Recommendations

1. Training

Agencies should tailor their training/educational programs on sexual harassment to the individual needs of each agency and ensure that they address the underlying issues discussed in this report. For training efforts to succeed, agencies must provide Federal employees with more than generic warnings that sexual harassment is improper. It must be clear that certain behavior can be deemed illegal and that sanctions can and will be applied to the responsible parties. In addition, however, the training should strive to increase the sensitivity of all parties as to the many faces of sexual harassment and what can be done informally as well as formally to reduce the incidence.

As an example of an innovative approach in this area, one Federal official responsible for a large installation took actions to halt sexual harassment that are similar to methods often used in the federal government to prevent alcohol and drug abuse. All managers and supervisors at this workplace were required to take sexual harassment training. Among those attending that training were employees with a history of sexually harassing behavior. These latter employees were notified by management that their attendance at training was required in a final effort to eliminate their prohibited behavior. They were informed that further sexual harassment of others on the job would result in a personnel action against them—including possible dismissal.

Aiming sexual harassment training at managers and personnel officials may have been appropriate initially, considering always-limited training resources, competing needs, and the imperative for initiating training focused on a problem newly recognized as serious in the federal workplace. However, in view of the continued high level of alleged sexual harassment in the government and increasing attention to the possible existence of a "hostile environment," agency training programs should also be broadened to include the entire work force.

Specifically, training should:

- Thoroughly cover the range of possible behaviors and the circumstances under which those behaviors may be considered sexual harassment; the formal and informal actions for seeking relief; the right to confidentiality under certain circumstances for those alleging harassment; the prohibition against reprisals; and current case law relevant to sexual harassment;

- Be provided to all employees, including nonsupervisory personnel. Also, training should enlighten all employees on their roles and responsibilities in preventing sexual harassment;

- Be quickly offered to new employees; and

- Be periodically evaluated for effectiveness. Agencies must be concerned with both the quantity and quality of sexual harassment training they offer. Managers should do a "quality control" review of their training efforts.

2. Policy Statements
Agencies should widely publicize a detailed list of specific actions that constitute sexual harassment, and penalties for each of the actions.
A Survey Respondent

Agencies should annually evaluate, modify, and reissue their policy statements on sexual harassment. Those statements should:

- Make it clear that sexual harassment is against the law and the agency will not tolerate it;

- Demonstrate the agency's commitment to the policy by issuing the statement under the signature of the agency head;

- Define the various behaviors that may constitute sexual harassment; this information should include a description of activities that may create a hostile environment (see the EEOC's guidelines on sexual harassment as a form of discrimination; see also, for example, the descriptions of verbal, nonverbal, and physical sexual harassment in the selection of policy state-

ments published in 1987 by the Bureau of National Affairs*);
and

- State the range of penalties the agency can levy against the
  offender, from warning to dismissal; discuss the possibility of
  personal liability for unlawful acts of harassment; and include
  reinforcing facts such as anecdotal or summary information on
  penalties already levied within the agency (or in other agencies) against sexual harassers.

3. Enforcement Action

I know my agency provides for swift investigations and disciplinary action for
sexual harassers and for supervisors who allow such misconduct to continue.

A Survey Respondent

**Agencies should establish strong and effective sanctions against sex-
ual harassment and issue penalties where appropriate.** Agencies
should, where possible, publicize to all employees the penalties
harassers face, from harassers who make submission a condition
or benefit of employment to those who contribute to creating an
offensive or hostile environment.

If policy statements treat penalties only in brief, such as by
giving only ranges or examples, agencies should make doubly sure
to publicize through additional means the complete array of penalties. Either way, agencies should ensure that all employees, including managers and supervisors, are given as complete and specific
information as possible.

4. Complaint and Investigation Procedures

In *Meritor, FSB v. Vinson* the Supreme Court found that the
"mere existence of a grievance procedure . . . and [a] policy
against discrimination . . . does not necessarily insulate the [em-
ployer] from liability." Also, the Court noted that the employer's
insulation "from liability might be substantially stronger if its

---

* Sexual Harassment: Employer Policies and Problems," PPF Survey No. 144, Wash., DC,
June 1987.

[grievance] procedures were better calculated to encourage victims of harassment to come forward."†

Agencies should post prominently the grievance procedures available for an individual who wishes to report sexual harassment.

A Survey Respondent

Agencies should review both the formal and informal avenues of redress available to employees who believe they are victims of sexual harassment and quickly institute any needed reforms. As a beginning, agencies should determine whether the process is timely and is otherwise appropriate for dealing with a sexual harassment allegation. As noted in *Meritor,* it is possible that liability on the part of an employer could be mitigated if the complaint process is tailored to accommodate charges of sexual harassment.

Agencies should review the ways in which they process formal complaints as part of a concerted effort to reduce the number of days it takes to resolve such complaints. A goal of 120 days is reasonable.

Agencies should widely publicize the institutionalized, or formal, complaint channels available, as well as the more informal actions employees may take, such as informing a supervisor. This publicity should clarify the way in which employees may use the formal channels, including how to contact the appropriate persons for assistance. Agencies should designate such personnel carefully, since a situation dealing with a charge of sexual harassment is highly charged and needs to be handled by a sensitive, knowledgeable person. It is particularly important for agencies to be sensitive to the need to designate employees of both sexes in whom victims can confide.**

As noted, employees view the effectiveness of agency actions less positively than agencies view them. This suggests that agencies need to instill more confidence in their employees with regard to agency concern about sexual harassment, determination to re-

---

† *Meritor Savings Bank v. Vinson,*106 S. Ct. 2399, 2409 (1986).

** In *Meritor,* at issue was that the bank's complaint procedure required a sexually harassed employee to report the incident to his or her supervisor. In this case, the alleged harasser was also the supervisor of the woman who believed she was a victim. The Court found that this complaint process was not tailored to accommodate the person charging sexual harassment.

duce its incidence, and commitment to strengthening procedures for dealing with it.

Ensuring that employees are fully aware of the alternatives available to them if they are harassed (and the specific steps to follow if they choose to pursue some type of action) can significantly help increase employees' confidence in their agencies' handling of sexual harassment.

Each agency should have a complaint process that gives employees confidence that the agency will (1) take sexual harassment allegations seriously, (2) handle them expeditiously, (3) strive for forceful and fair resolution, (4) enforce penalties against harassers, and (5) not tolerate reprisals.

5. Additional Prevention Efforts

Prevention efforts could include periodic random, anonymous surveys to determine whether sexual harassment is a problem in a given agency, department, or office within that agency. An evaluation/prevention effort could include conducting periodic followup interviews with all personnel involved in the settlement of both informal and formal complaints. These interviews would allow management to assess the current work environment of the employees involved to ensure that problems relating to that sexual harassment incident were no longer extant.

Conclusion

MSPB recognizes that the complete absence of behaviors that some consider sexual harassment may not be possible. However, we believe agency heads must make it clear they are taking a "zero tolerance level" approach to sexual harassment in their workplaces. We also believe that implementation of the recommendations in this report will result in a significant, long-term reduction in the incidence of sexual harassment.

3. What are the procedures if a federal employee chooses to file a sexual harassment complaint?

a) First, the complainant must consult with an Equal Employment Opportunity counselor at the employing federal agency within 30 days of the alleged act. The EEO counselor will conduct an inquiry and attempt to resolve the complaint informally.

b) If the matter is not resolved within 21 days of contacting the EEO counselor, you may file a complaint with the employing agency.

c) If the employing agency accepts the complaint, it institutes an investigation.

d) If the employing agency does not accept the complaint you then have the right to appeal to the EEOC's Review and Appeals Department.

4. How is the complaint investigated?

—Affidavits are taken from you and other witnesses. You are given a copy of the results of the investigation. Informal resolution of the dispute is still possible.

5. Are you entitled to a hearing?

—Yes. The agency will notify you of its proposed final decision. If you are not satisfied with the proposed final decision, you may request a hearing but must do so within 15 days of your learning of the proposed final decision.

6. Who conducts the hearing?

—An EEOC administrative judge.

7. What happens at the hearing?

—Testimony is taken. Witnesses are cross-examined and documents are examined.

8. Is the administrative judge's judgment final?

—No. It is a recommended decision that your employing agency can accept, reject or modify.

9. If you are not satisfied with the decision of the employing agency what can you do?

—You can appeal the decision to the EEOC's Review and Appeal office, but must do so within 30 days of the receipt of the decision.

10. Can a federal employee file a lawsuit in federal court?

—Yes.

11. When can the suit be commenced?

a) Within 30 days of receipt of final action by the employing agency or within 30 days of receipt of EEOC final action on your appeal or

b) After 180 days from filing a complaint if there has been no decision by your agency or after 180 days from filing an appeal with the EEOC if no decision has been revealed.

SECTION 7: EDUCATIONAL INSTITUTIONS

1. Is sexual harassment of students in academia illegal?

Yes. It is a violation of Title VII of the 1964 Civil Rights Act and Title IX of the 1972 Education Amendments. Title VII is explained in previous sections of this book. Title IX bars discrimination by any recipient of federal funds. Most colleges and universities are recipients of federal funds.

2. What is sexual harassment in academia?
   —It consists of many different types of behavior from sexual statements to unwanted sexual advances to sexual bribery (rewards for sex) and sexual coercion. It generally refers to harassment of students by faculty or other university employees.

3. Is sexual harassment in academia commonplace?
   —Yes. Studies have indicated that 30% to 50% of female undergraduates experience sexual harassment.

4. What should a student do if sexually harassed?
   —Advise the harasser in writing of the unacceptability of his/her conduct and keep a copy of the letter. If this is not successful, advise the educational institution of your grievance and utilize grievance procedures or your legal remedies.

5. Can a student sexually harass a professor?
   —Yes, however this occurs less frequently and would be subject to the university's disciplinary procedures rather than federal law.

6. Do most educational institutions have policies on sexual harassment and grievance procedures?
   —Yes. If yours does not you should work for the adoption of both a policy on sexual harassment and a grievance procedure.

7. What are some examples of university policies on sexual harassment?
   A) Harvard Policy

Questions and Answers

The following letter from Dean Henry Rosovsky was sent to every faculty member and student in the Faculty of Arts and Sciences at Harvard University (MA). In it, Dean Rosovsky discusses the subtle and for the most part unintentional faculty behaviors which alienate or discourage women students; relationships between faculty members and students which are considered not only unprofessional but wrong in an instructional context; and university policies and procedures for dealing with complaints of sexual harassment.

The Dean's letter reflects a trend at colleges and universities across the country to develop more formal written policies and guidelines regarding sexual harassment and the subtle and potential discrimination that women students still face on campus. For example, in November 1983, the University of California's Assembly of the Academic Senate adopted a proposal to ban sex between teachers and their students stating that even "consenting" relationships can inflict "irreparable" damage to the educational environment. Such relationships are considered a "serious breach of professional ethics," even if initiated by a student. The ban, which applies only to students directly under a teacher's supervision, either in a class or while doing research, does not carry any penalty for those who refuse to follow it. However, it is a standard for professional conduct. Institutions are increasingly mindful of the need to clarify and formalize just such standards of behavior for the benefit of their faculty and their students.

The following statement is not intended as a model for use at every college and university but as one way of many in which the subject of sexual harassment and related issues can be publicized. In addition, institutions will need to develop and assess procedures for dealing with complaints about these issues. Institutions may also want to mention in these policy statements that sexual harassment violates Title IX and other laws as well. Furthermore, an institution may find it helpful to inform its academic community as to the steps it has taken when formal procedures are completed. It is hoped that many colleges and universities will initiate discussions of the prob-

lem and develop policies on their own campuses to ensure that women's experience on campus will be as positive and as conducive to learning as that of their brothers.

April 1983

Dear Colleague:

During the current academic year, the Faculty Council has been discussing the topic of sexual harassment. This conversation arose because students and faculty members have questioned whether we have fair and effective procedures for responding to complaints, and whether we have a good working definition of the term "sexual harassment."

In the course of discussion, the Faculty Council took up a number of related topics, particularly the complex question of appropriate and inappropriate relationships between students and faculty members, and the question of sex as it may affect the teaching environment. I am writing to you now to report on the substance of these discussions and to review for you the understandings reached by the Faculty Council on these various interrelated topics.

I shall comment first on the environment of the classroom, particularly certain difficulties that can arise between instructors and the students enrolled in their classes, collectively rather than individually. Second, I shall discuss certain difficulties that may arise in the relationships between individual instructors and individual students. Third, I shall describe what kinds of behavior on the part of faculty members will produce formal disciplinary action. Finally, I shall outline the disciplinary procedures for responding to such behavior.

1. The teaching environment

In the last decade we have made considerable progress toward a genuinely co-educational environment. Overt discrimination against women seems to be quite rare. Most members of the faculty endeavor to treat all students fairly as individuals, and not as members of a category based on sex.

Nevertheless we have not yet attained a state in which women never feel themselves to be disadvantaged on account of their sex. Students continue to report behavior by members of the teaching staff that is discouraging or offensive to women. Alienating messages may be subtle and even unintentional. It may therefore be useful to offer specific examples illustrating a range of classroom conduct that tends to compromise the learning experience especially, but not only, of women.

Some teaching practices are overtly hostile to women. For example, to "show slides of nude women humorously or whimsically" during an otherwise serious lecture is not only in poor taste, but is also demeaning to women.

Other alienating teaching practices may be simply thoughtless, and may even be the result of special efforts to be helpful to women students. It is condescending to make a point of calling upon women in class on topics such as marriage and the family, imposing the assumption that only women have a "natural" interest in this area.

There is no specific term for the classroom practices just described. Their common effect is to focus attention on sex characteristics in a context in which sex would otherwise be irrelevant. For that reason, the general term "sexism" is often used to describe this category of unprofessional behavior.

2. Relationships between individual faculty members and students

The Council discussed various kinds of personal relationships between faculty members and students. Members of the Council generally agreed that, in addition to the harassing behavior described below, certain other kinds of relationships are wrong whenever they take place within an instructional context.

Amorous relationships that might be appropriate in other circumstances are always wrong when they occur between any teacher or officer of the university and any student for whom he or she has a professional responsibility. Further, such relationships may have the effect of undermining the atmosphere of trust on which the educational process depends. Implicit in the idea of professionalism is the recognition by those in positions of authority that in their relationships with students there is always an element of power. It is incumbent upon those with authority not to abuse, nor to seem to abuse, the power with which they are entrusted.

Officers and other members of the teaching staff should be aware that any romantic involvement with their students makes them liable for formal action against them if a complaint is initiated by a student. Even when both parties have consented to the development of such a relationship, it is the officer or instructor who, by virtue of his or her special responsibility, will be held accountable for unprofessional behavior. Because graduate student teaching fellows, tutors, and undergraduate course assistants may be less accustomed than faculty members to thinking of themselves as holding professional responsibilities, they would be wise to exercise special care in their relationships with students whom they instruct or evaluate.

Other amorous relationships between members of the faculty and students, occurring outside the instructional context, may also lead to difficulties. In a personal relationship between an officer and a student for whom the officer has no current professional responsibility, the officer should be sensitive to the constant possibility that he or she may unexpectedly be placed in a position of responsibility for the student's instruction or evaluation. Relationships between officers and students are always fundamentally asymmetric in nature.

3. Sexual harassment

The Faculty Council accepts the following definition of sexual harassment:

In the academic context, the term "sexual harassment" may be used to describe a wide range of behavior. The fundamental element is the inappropriate personal attention by an instructor or other officer who is in a position to determine a student's grade or otherwise affect the student's academic performance or professional future. Such behavior is unacceptable in a university because it is a form of unprofessional behavior which seriously undermines the atmosphere of trust essential to the academic enterprise.

The faculty's procedures for responding to complaints of sexual harassment provide three routes through which complaints can be resolved. In consultation with the Assistant Dean of Harvard College (or, in the case of a graduate student, an appropriate officer as outlined in the GSAS procedures,) the student selects the most suitable process, which will ordinarily depend on the nature of the instructor's behavior and the form of redress sought by the student.

In the least formal approach, the Assistant Dean (or the Director of the Office of Student Affairs of GSAS) provides help in resolving the difficulty. (Examples of informal resolutions include apologies and changes in instructional arrangements. Such readjustments of the teacher-student relationship are likely to be adequate responses only in those cases in which miscommunication or lack of communication played a significant part.)

Through the faculty's formal process, a student may seek disciplinary action by the Dean of the Faculty against the instructor. The formal process is intended to react to conduct that is clearly understood to be unacceptable. The underlying assumption is that all members of the faculty are aware that it is wrong to expect sexual favors of one's students, and that persistent, unwanted attention by an instructor toward a student is always, therefore, unprofessional.

The faculty's formal procedure is confidential. Officers of the university do not comment publicly on individual cases. Nevertheless the university cannot ordinarily prevent the parties to a complaint from discussing it publicly.

The third route is considerably more elaborate than the other two. Screening and Hearing Panels are available to consider charges of "grave misconduct," identified in the Third Statute of the University as grounds for termination of employment, including deprivation of tenure.

In addition, the Administrative Board of Harvard and Radcliffe Colleges and the Administrative Board of the Graduate School are available to provide certain kinds of help to students who have been the victims of sexual harassment. The Administrative Board considers students' petitions for changes of grading status (that is, from letter-graded to pass-fail) and petitions for retroactive withdrawals from courses. Such petitions are granted on account of special circumstances, in which category the Board would ordinarily include clear instances of sexual harassment.

I have given an account of the Faculty Council's thinking on the topic of sexual harassment and related issues. The Council did not reach unanimity on every detail of the views expressed in this letter, but the Council did support this general approach to the problem and reaffirmed its confidence in our current procedures for responding to specific instances of sexual harassment.

I have written this letter so that every member of the faculty might be aware of these discussions, and of my own views. If members of the faculty feel that this statement is incomplete, or incorrect in some way, I would be grateful if they would write to me.

Sincerely yours,
Henry Rosovsky

B) Iowa Policy

The University of Iowa has adopted a new policy which not only prohibits sexual harassment of students, but also forbids faculty-student romantic relationships, even when both parties have apparently consented to the relationship. The policy also defines sexual harassment and gives examples of prohibited activities including sexist jokes and sexist remarks "including a pattern of conduct (not legitimately related to the subject matter of a course if one is involved) intended to discomfort or humiliate, or both." That portion of the policy dealing with consensual relationships is as follows:

DIVISION 2. CONSENSUAL RELATIONSHIPS

Section 5. *Definition*
As used in this Division, the terms "faculty" or "faculty member" mean all those who teach at the university, and include

graduate students with teaching responsibilities and other instructional personnel.

Section 6. *Rationale*

(a) The university's educational mission is promoted by professionalism in faculty-student relationships. Professionalism is fostered by an atmosphere of mutual trust and respect. Actions of faculty members and students that harm this atmosphere undermine professionalism and hinder fulfillment of the university's educational mission. Trust and respect are diminished when those in positions of authority abuse, or appear to abuse, their power. Those who abuse, or appear to abuse, their power in such a context violate their duty to the university community.

(b) Faculty members exercise power over students, whether in giving them praise or criticism, evaluating them, making recommendations for their further studies or their future employment, or conferring any other benefits on them. Amorous relationships between faculty members and students are wrong when the faculty member has professional responsibility for the student. Such situations greatly increase the chances that the faculty member will abuse his or her power and sexually exploit the student. Voluntary consent by the student in such a relationship is suspect, given the fundamentally asymmetric nature of the relationship. Moreover, other students and faculty may be affected by such unprofessional behavior because it places the faculty member in a position to favor or advance one student's interest at the expense of others and implicitly makes obtaining benefits contingent on amorous or sexual favors. Therefore, the university will view it as unethical if faculty members engage in amorous relations with students enrolled in their classes or subject to their supervision, even when both parties appear to have consented to the relationship.

Section 7. *Consensual Relationships in the Instructional Context*

No faculty member shall have an amorous relationship (consensual or otherwise) with a student who is enrolled in a course being taught by the faculty member or whose academic work (including work as a teaching assistant) is being supervised by the faculty member.

Section 8. *Consensual Relationships Outside the Instructional Context*
Amorous relationships between faculty members and students occurring outside the instructional context may lead to difficulties. Particularly when the faculty member and student are in the same academic unit or in units that are academically allied, relationships that the parties view as consensual may appear to others to be exploitative. Further, in such situations (and others that cannot be anticipated), the faculty member may face serious conflicts of interest and should be careful to distance himself or herself from any decisions that may reward or penalize the student involved. The faculty member who fails to withdraw from participation in activities or decisions that may reward or penalize a student with whom the faculty member has or has had an amorous relationship will be deemed to have violated his or her ethical obligation to the student, to other students, to colleagues, and to the university.

8. Are all educational institutions covered by Title IX required to maintain grievance procedures for resolution of sexual harassment complaints?
    —Yes. It is required by the office of Civil Rights in the Department of Education.

9. What does this mean for educational institutions?
    —Institutions should have both policy statements and grievance procedures on issues of sexual harassment. In addition the U.S. Merit Systems Protection Board in 1981 stated that

specific additional procedures are needed to address sexual harassment. These include:

a) A memorandum from its president condemning sexual harassment distributed to all.

b) Materials educating people as to their rights in sexual harassment cases should be distributed to all.

10. Can a student sue for damages for sexual harassment?
—Yes. In a 9–0 decision in 1992 the Supreme Court ruled that Title IX of the 1972 Education Amendments did authorize monetary damages.

11. Do the EEOC Guidelines apply to educational institutions?
—Yes. These guidelines are in chapter five.

12. If a professor implies that you might receive better grades if you have a date with him, is he or she engaging in sexual harassment?
—Yes.

13. If a professor repeatedly asks you for a date is he or she engaging in a form of sexual harassment?
—Yes.

14. If a professor shows favoritism to a student of the opposite sex do you have a grievance?
—Yes, if you are not receiving equal treatment.

15. Do some educational institutions ban sexual relationships between students and faculty?
    —Yes.

16. If the educational institution does not have effective policies and procedures on sexual harassment may a student sue the educational institution?
    —Yes.

17. May a student sue the educational institution for sexual harassment by a professor?
    —Yes. The educational institution is responsible if it knew or should have known or if it did too little to resolve the charges.

18. Where there is sexual harassment in an educational institution, can the institution lose its federal assistance?
    —Yes.

19. If I am sexually harassed should I keep a written record?
    —Yes, with the date, time, place, witnesses and description of the sexual harassment.

Chapter 4

NOW Legal Resource Kit

Overview of Federal Sexual Harassment Law*

INTRODUCTION

If you believe that you are being sexually harassed you should know about the federal, state and local laws which exist to protect you. This resource kit describes the federal law that give you rights to sue your employer for sexual harassment.

In addition to federal law, every state and many cities and towns have their own equal employment laws which in some cases give you more rights and remedies and more favorable procedures. Check with your state and local departments of employment/human rights/human relations for information on the scope and existence of other helpful equal employment laws in your area. This resource kit contains a listing of each state's equal employment agencies where sexual harassment claims are filed. Additional state and city numbers should be in your telephone directory. Additional actions under your state workers' compensation or personal injury laws may be available if the harassment causes you either emotional or physical injury. You may wish to consult a law-

* The Civil Rights Act of 1991 contains a number of changes in the federal law which are not reflected in this chapter but which are discussed in Chapter 3.

yer, licensed to practice law in your geographical area, who specializes in workers' compensation and personal injury law about the possibility of initiating these types of suits. If the harassment involved physical touching, coerced physical confinement or coerced sex acts, you may also have suffered from a criminal act prohibited by state law and you may want to contact your local law enforcement agencies.

This packet is not a substitute for a lawyer's advice but it does provide useful information to help you stand up for your federally protected rights.

RELEVANT FEDERAL LEGISLATION

Title VII of the Civil Rights Act of 1964

Title VII of the Civil Rights Act prohibits sexual harassment in the workplace. Sexual harassment is any unwelcome sexual attention or harassment, even if not specifically sexual, which is directed only at one sex. Examples of sexual harassment by co-workers and/or supervisors are sexual advances, comments on your body, sex life, or sexual preference, touching, grabbing, telling sexual jokes, the display of pornography at the workplace, or making comments like "women belong in the bedroom or kitchen, not at work." Sexual harassment also includes a specific request for sex by your supervisor combined with direct or indirect threats of negative consequences for your job if you refuse.

You do not have to tolerate sexual harassment from your boss or co-workers. If the harassment is so severe that it interferes with your job performance, or it makes you feel intimidated, scared or stressed, it may constitute a violation of your equal employment rights under Title VII. An isolated incident of general sexual harassment by co-workers and/or supervisors does not usually constitute a violation of Title VII (unless the incident is extreme, like assault or rape). Whether you can win a sexual harassment lawsuit depends on whether the incidents complained of are severe enough or numerous enough to bother a reasonable woman. However, even one request for sex tied to your job by your boss may be enough to prove a Title VII violation.

Whether or not you could win a federal lawsuit based on your situation, *every employer is under a duty to stamp out sexual harassment* and you have every right to expect the employer to fulfill that duty. In this resource kit you will find a pamphlet to help you get your employer to do so, entitled "Guidelines for Advocates: Effective Complaint and Investigation Procedures for Workplace Sexual Harassment."

Under Title VII you cannot sue your co-workers for sexual harassment. However, you can sue your employer (company) and high level supervisors for the harassing and discriminatory actions of your supervisors, or for knowingly allowing your co-workers to continually harass you and make the workplace a hostile environment.

You are not required to ignore individual incidents until they build up to be so intolerable that you must leave your job or suffer severe mental anguish. If an incident of sexual harassment occurs, you should make it clear to the harasser that you do not welcome his behavior and you want it to stop. A sample "letter to a harasser" is included in this kit. If you do not feel comfortable confronting the harasser, consider speaking with your or the harasser's supervisor. Your legal claims may be hurt if you keep silent instead of informing the harasser and/or your employer or supervisor that you do not welcome such behavior. You should keep records of all conversations about the harassment since your employer may later try to deny that you notified them. Also, by informing your supervisor or employer of the harassment, you put your employer on notice so that if you bring a claim you are able to sue your employer for failure to stop the harassment.

Your employer may have a sexual harassment policy and/or a confidential procedure for investigating and resolving sexual harassment claims. However, if you can show that the complaint procedure is a sham or that it will only expose you to greater harm —for example if you have to complain to your harasser or his friends—it should not hurt your legal claim if you did not use the in-house grievance procedure. Using an in-house grievance procedure does not mean that you have lost your right to bring a later complaint with a city, state or federal agency if the complaint was not resolved satisfactorily through the company's procedure. Of course sorting out any problem without the bother of formal action is preferable. In talking to people at your workplace to try to solve the problem, remember that you may not have a legal claim *or* you may have a claim but decide not to pursue it for any variety of reasons. For example, a suit or EEOC complaint may be too costly, too risky, too damaging to your personal life, or may not offer the sort of outcome you desire. In the course of asking for the help you need, it is therefore probably smart not to punctuate your requests with "or I'll sue you!" One special note: even if a lawsuit is too costly for you alone, you may discover, as you attempt to solve the problem informally, that others have suffered too and could share expenses and be added to the claim either by name, or anonymously as members of a group of people who have been similarly treated if there are enough of you.

What should you do if you feel you are being harassed?

If you think you are being harassed you should begin to keep notes. Write down the date, time, what happened, the players and names of any witnesses to the harassment. Note down also if you lost any money as a result, for example by having to take a day off. Keep your notes in a safe place at home separated from personal diaries and records. If your employer keeps written records about your job performance and you have a good employment record, send a sealed copy of your employment records to yourself and do not open the envelope. It may be useful evidence regarding the state of your record at the time of delivery and it will be safe from loss or tampering.

If you feel safe in doing so, talk to sympathetic co-workers who may become potential witnesses or co-plaintiffs. Keep any notes, cards, or presents your harasser gives you as evidence. If you are a union member, you may consider contacting your local representative or shop steward and following the grievance procedures outlined in the contract.

If you wish to file a complaint about the harassment you should contact the nearest Equal Employment Opportunity Commission (EEOC) office and/or the human rights agency which enforces your state and/or city equal employment laws. There is no fee for filing and the agency does not charge for either investigating or attempting to resolve your complaint. Your complaint should include all instances of harassment and the names of all responsible individuals.

The telephone number and address of your nearest EEOC branch office should be in the resource kit's list or in your telephone directory. If not, call 1-800-USA-EEOC or write to: Equal Employment Opportunity Commission, 2401 E Street, N.W., Washington, D.C. 20506. When talking to federal and local agencies concerning discrimination or civil rights violations, find out the requirements for filing a claim. Request a description of the process in writing. The following is a suggestion of the questions you should consider asking:

—Where and with whom do I file?

—What is the time limit within which I must file?

—What is the process once I have filed? (For the EEOC) If I file with you, do you investigate my claim or do you send it over to the state agency to investigate? If you send it to the state, does that have any effect on rights I may have under state law?

—(For state/city agencies) If I file with you do I lose my right to bring my case in state court?

Be very careful to take note of the time limits required by these agencies, because if you do not comply with these limits your complaint may be dismissed. Do not delay in contacting them because they will only accept complaints about harassment that is still happening or happened from 180 to 300 days ago (depending on the agency).

The agency process is designed for people to use without a lawyer and without large expenditures of time and money. There is no fee for filing. Your complaint should describe all the types of harassment you have suffered and include all the supervisors who took part or failed to stop the co-worker harassment. The agency notifies your employer of your complaint, investigates it and attempts to resolve the problem. At the end of the investigation, the

EEOC sends you either a "right to sue" letter or notification that they intend to bring the case on your behalf by initiating a suit in federal court. If the EEOC litigates the case on your behalf, you do not pay them for their efforts and you may receive monetary damages, such as back pay and reinstatement.

A "right to sue" letter means that the EEOC will not bring the case on your behalf. This is far more common. The letter will indicate whether or not the EEOC believes that discrimination took place, but even if the EEOC does not believe it, you may still go to court to try to prove it there. If you wish to initiate a sexual harassment lawsuit you must do so on your own. Because court procedures and deadlines are stricter and more complex, it is probably best to be represented by an attorney, preferably one familiar with sexual harassment law. One problem with bringing your own case is that lawyers are expensive. Very little federal funding exists to pay for free legal representation for people with sexual harassment cases. However, if your income is less than 125 percent of the federal poverty level, you may be able to get free legal services from the Legal Aid Society or a Legal Services Corporation in your area.

Additionally, you may be able to retain an attorney for either no fee or a small down payment with an agreement that if you win in court the attorney will seek an award of reasonable attorney's fees from your employer as provided in the applicable federal, state or local discrimination laws and/or receive a predetermined percentage of any money you win. In addition, since Title VII was amended by the Civil Rights Act of 1991, if you win your sex discrimination case you may be able to make the employer pay you for the pain and suffering the discrimination caused (compensatory damages), and possibly an additional amount to punish the employer if you can show that the employer deliberately planned to discriminate against you or acted without caring whether or not you would suffer when it was obvious that you would suffer (punitive damages). Unfortunately, there is currently a limit on the amount of compensatory and punitive damages that you can win in even the worst cases. The limit depends on how many employees the employer has. The limits are as follows: If your company has 100 or fewer employees, the total for compensatory and punitive damages combined is $50,000. If your company has 200 or fewer employees, the combined total is $100,000. If your company has 500 or fewer employees, the combined total is $200,000. If there are more than 500 employees in your company, the combined total is $300,000. None of this money is payable in cases where the discrimination takes the form of a neutral policy and the employer did not mean it to discriminate. Either a judge, or a jury if you or the employer asks for one, decides on the amount of damages within the limits that the employer has to pay you if you win. Your state laws on equal employment opportunity, contracts or torts, under which you may have additional rights, may also give you damages.

Most lawyers, even if they don't charge hourly fees until you win, require that you cover the "costs," *e.g.,* filing and witness fees, deposition and transcript fees, copying, telephone calls and other out-of-pocket expenses. Make sure if you agree to do this that you have a good understanding of how much this may add up to. In sum, a lawsuit will be an investment of money as well as time.

To locate a lawyer, you can begin by asking your acquaintances for a possible referral. Most state bar associations provide lawyer referral services. To locate your local bar association, look in the telephone directory under the name of the county, city, or state. You can also write to the Public Education Division, American Bar Association, 750 N. Lake Shore Drive, Chicago, Illinois 60611, for a copy of "The American Lawyer: When and How to Use One," a publication of the American Bar Association. Additionally, if your case raises precedent setting issues for women or a particularly difficult point of law, the following organizations may be able to help you find an attorney to represent you:

Trial Lawyers for Public Justice
1625 Massachusetts Avenue, N.W.
Suite 100
Washington, D.C. 20036

National Employment Lawyers' Association
911 Mercantile Library Bldg.
414 Walnut Street
Cincinnati, Ohio 45202

National Lawyers Guild
55 Avenue of the Americas
New York, New York 10013

NOW Legal Defense and Education Fund
99 Hudson Street
12th Floor
New York, New York 10013

When you find a lawyer, give them the publication, "Sexual Harassment in the Workplace Litigation," which is enclosed in this kit.

Support Groups

You are your own best witness and best resource. But you are not alone. If you are facing a harassment problem get yourself some support. Join a support group of women in your profession or job or one with other women who have suffered sexual harassment in the workplace. Joining a general women's group could also give you support. The following organizations have support and action groups open to women nationwide:

National Organization for Women
1000 16th Street, N.W.
Suite 700
Washington, D.C. 20036

National Black Women's Health Project
1237 Gordon Street, S.W.
Atlanta, Georgia 30310

Good Luck!

DEFINING SEXUAL HARASSMENT

The term "sexual harassment" encompasses a broad range of unwelcome acts that focus on women's* sexuality, rather than on their contributions as employees. Sexual harassment also includes harassment, not sexual in nature, that would not occur but for the sex of the employee. These acts may be visual (such as leering, ogling and physical gestures conveying a visual meaning), verbal (derogatory remarks and innuendos, jokes and outright verbal abuse) or physical (from pinching and fondling to rape). Sexual harassment also includes requests for sexual relations combined with explicit or implicit threats of adverse job consequences if the woman refuses. Under the Equal Employment Opportunity Commission (EEOC) guidelines sexual harassment is defined as follows:

> Unwelcome sexual advances, requests for sexual favors, and other verbal or physical conduct of a sexual nature constitute sexual harassment when (1) submission to such conduct is made either explicitly or implicitly a term or condition of an individual's employment, (2) submission to, or rejection of such conduct by an individual is used as the basis for employment decisions affecting such individual, or (3) such conduct has the purpose or effect of unreasonably interfering with an individual's work performance or creating an intimidating, hostile, or offensive working environment. 29 C.F.R. 1604.11(a) (1987).

This is probably the best working definition of sexual harassment. Sexual harassment as a concept encompasses the full range of coercive behavior from subtle psychological force to gross physical abuse.

The courts have recognized two forms of sexual harassment claims under Title VII of the Civil Rights Act of 1964: the "quid

---

* Although both males and females can be and are sexually harassed, we characterize the victims of sexual harassment as female because women are harassed much more frequently than men.

pro quo" claim, and the "hostile environment" claim. The quid pro quo claim (literally "this for that") involves harassment in which a supervisory employee demands sexual favors in exchange for job benefits over which that supervisor has some control or influence. By conditioning some aspect of employment on submission to sexual demands, the supervisory employee imposes on females an additional burden as a prerequisite to employment which men need not suffer, and the employer may be sued for this action of its agent.

The hostile work environment claim involves unwelcome behavior of a sexual nature which creates an intimidating, hostile, or offensive work environment or has the effect of unreasonably interfering with an individual's work performance. Although the quid pro quo claim is limited to harassment by one with authority to make substantive employment decisions (e.g., a supervisor with authority to hire, fire, promote, etc.), the hostile environment claim includes unwelcome behavior of a sexual nature by anyone in the workplace, if the employer or its agents know or reasonably should have known about the harassing conditions regardless of who created those conditions. The taxonomy of quid pro quo and hostile work environment cases describes categories of behavior that fall on a continuum and not into clearly separate and distinct divisions.

SAMPLE "LETTER TO A HARASSER"

Date

Dear Harasser
I am writing this letter to inform you that I do not welcome and have been made to feel (uncomfortable) (intimidated) (threatened) (angered) by your action(s). The action(s) I am referring to is (include):

Examples

At the office's 1991 Christmas party, telling me that I could go far in the company if I was a "good sport" and a "team player" —proving this by sleeping with you.

On or around July 24, 1991, leaving a magazine on my desk that I consider obscene, opened to the centerfold. When I asked if it were yours, you claimed that you thought that I would be interested in the subject.

On three separate occasions, starting on the second day of my employment, following me into the supply closet to hug me and fondle my breasts.

On numerous occasions, standing around my desk to speculate with Joe Chauvinist about my possible sexual practices.

Booking only one hotel room for the two of us at the engineering association conference in Phoenix and changing the reservation only after I insisted in front of the clerk. At the banquet that evening you told me that I was "jeopardizing our working relationship and my position" with my "unfriendliness."

This behavior is offensive to me and constitutes sexual harassment. This (these) incident(s) has (have) created a (unprofessional) (tense) (stressful) (detrimental) (harmful) working environment that interferes with my job performance, particularly in any matters that require contact with you. Therefore, I am asking you to stop this illegal harassment now.

Optional Paragraph
If you continue with this behavior, or harass me further as a result of this letter, I will deliver a copy of this letter to (your supervisor,_____) (the Personnel Department) (my union representative) (the president of the company,_____). **[NOTE: use the steps of the employer's grievance procedure, if any such procedure exists.]** If necessary, I will file a formal complaint with the (Equal Employment Opportunity Commission) (state or local Fair Em-

ployment Practices agency), which investigates charges of employment discrimination.

Sincerely

Harassee

(cc:_____)
(encl, e.g. *copies* of notes)

be sure to make copies of your letter!

SEXUAL HARASSMENT IN THE WORKPLACE LITIGATION[*]

I. GROUNDS OF ACTION FOR SEXUAL HARASSMENT

A. Title VII of the Civil Rights Act of 1964, 42 U.S.C.§2000e et seq.

Sexual harassment is now commonly understood to be sex discrimination under Title VII. *See Meritor Savings Bank v. Vinson,* 477 U.S. 57 (1986).

1. Proving Title VII sexual harassment: The Elements.
The accepted definition of sexual harassment is set forth in the EEOC Guidelines at 29 C.F.R. §1604.11(a):

Unwelcome sexual advances, requests for sexual favors, and other verbal or physical conduct of a sexual nature constitute sexual harassment when (1) submission to such conduct is made either explicitly or implicitly a term or condition of an individual's employment, (2) submission to or rejection of such conduct by an individual is used as the basis for employment decisions affecting such individual, or (3) such conduct has the purpose or effect of unreasonably interfering with an

[*] this outline is prepared to provide guidance for the plaintiff's counsel on developing legal issues in the area of sexual harassment under Title VII. This piece is premised upon the assumption that the user has access to resources on the old caselaw in the area. It is a work in progress.

individual's work performance or creating an intimidating, hostile, or offensive working environment.

Meeting the elements of a. "unwelcomeness," b. words or acts of a sexual nature, and c. any one of three conditions of injury makes out a claim of sexual harassment. This definition is more complicated but also more effective than the popular dichotomization of harassment into so-called "quid pro quo," *e.g., Barnes v. Costle,* 561 F.2d 983 (D.C. Cir. 1977) (failure to accede to supervisor's sexual demands results in tangible job detriment) and "hostile environment," *Bundy v. Jackson,* 641 F.2d 934 (D.C. Cir. 1981) (sexual harassment not affecting economic benefits that creates a hostile or offensive working environment is an unlawful discriminatory term or condition of employment under Title VII). The problem with the quid pro quo/hostile environment dichotomy is that it minimizes the extent to which sexually harassing acts fall upon a continuum encompassing both, simultaneously or over time. For example, as a female employee responds to her hostile work environment in any of a variety of ways (e.g. complaining), the employer or its agents may impose job detriments upon her such as transfer, demotion, firing, non-promotion (for example, on the alleged ground that "she can't get along"). Also, as a supervisor makes quid pro quo demands on any one female he may create an environment hostile to all females. Sometimes the same or similar facts should be characterized as sexual harassment *and* retaliation; a court may not see job detriments as having been imposed because a woman refused the sexual harassment but may see it as retaliation after she resisted discrimination. The possibility that quid pro quo and environment claims are not strictly dichotomous may be important to recognize in addressing agency "respondeat superior" requirements for liability, as well. Having made this cautionary note, this discussion divides the "proof of harm" section c. below along the lines of the so-called elements of proving "quid pro quo" and "hostile environment" because the cases have taken that approach.

a. Unwelcomeness.

The threshold standard is whether the alleged sexual acts were "unwelcome"; Title VII does not outlaw consensual sexual relations and accordingly the EEOC Guidelines imposed an unwelcomeness standard. The plaintiff bears the burden of pleading and proving unwelcomeness. The fact that the alleged harasser and victim had a consensual relationship is not *per se* fatal to a claim. Even if the complaining party is found to have "voluntarily" entered into a relationship, a case of sexual harassment may still be made with respect to the unwelcome acts. *Meritor Savings Bank v. Vinson,* 477 U.S. 57 (1986). The problem in the "voluntary" association case is credibility of the plaintiff on the issue of unwelcomeness. *See, e.g., Sardigal v. St. Louis National Stockyards Co.,* 42 F.E.P. Cases 497 (S.D.Ill. 1986) (voluntary association with alleged harassing co-worker showed plaintiff "welcomed, if not encouraged" sexual remarks, etc.); *Bouchet v. National Urban League,* 33 F.E.P. Cases 536 (D.D.C. 1982), *aff'd,* 730 F.2d 799 (D.C. Cir. 1984) (court found, *inter alia,* that plaintiff was not unaware that attraction was a factor in her hiring and she did nothing to discourage it); EEOC Dec. No. 84-1, 33 F.E.P. Cases 1887 (11/23/83) (participating in offensive atmosphere by telling "dirty jokes" defeats claim of unwelcomeness). NOTE: Expert testimony may be needed to explain how and why women "participate in," in other words, accommodate to an atmosphere or quid pro quo treatment. On unwelcomeness, *see also Katz v. Dole,* 709 F.2d 251 (4th Cir. 1983) (banter with friend at work does not waive right to nondiscrimination).

b. Sexual Advances, Requests for Sexual Favors, and Other Verbal or Physical Conduct of a Sexual Nature

In the period between 1974–1980 the federal courts struggled with the perception of sexual harassment as "sex discrimination" and some dismissed it as being "personal" or reflecting the individual proclivities of the harasser. That view was rejected by the federal courts and the EEOC Guidelines were written to indicate clearly that "sexual advances, requests for sexual favors, and other verbal or physical conduct of a sexual nature" would be "sex discrimination."

(1) Sexual harassment is arguably "facial" discrimination. The sexual content of the sexually harassing words and actions make the action "facially discriminatory" or on their face based upon sex, *see Henson v. City of Dundee*, 682 F.2d 897, 905 n. 11 (11th Cir. 1982). *Cf. Priced Waterhouse v. Hopkins*, 490 U.S. _____, 109 S.Ct. 1775 2D 104 L.Ed 2D 268, (1989) (using sex stereotypic evaluations as basis for promotion denial); *Dothard v. Rawlinson*, 433 U.S. 321 (1977) (hiring men but not women for employment as prison security guards); *Phillips v. Martin Marietta*, 400 U.S. 542 (1971) (excluding women but not men with preschool aged children from employment); *Carroll v. Talman Federal Sav. & Loan Ass'n*, 604 F.2d 1025 (7th Cir. 1979), *cert. denied*, 445 U.S. 929 (1980) (requiring only female employees to wear uniforms was "disparate treatment . . . demeaning to women . . . based on offensive stereotypes prohibited by Title VII").

(2) Moreover, harassing conduct that follows a pattern of sex-based disparate treatment is also discriminatory even if not "sexual" in nature. The most common mode of proof of discrimination is "disparate treatment" proof, i.e. that a female is being treated differently than a similarly situated male. Accordingly, any harassing treatment, whether sexual in nature or not, could come within a Title VII sexual harassment analysis. *See, e.g., Hicks v. Gates Rubber Co.*, 833 F.2d 1406 (10th Cir. 1987) (threatening bellicose, demeaning hostile conduct "harassing" if sex-based even if not sexually suggestive); *Bell v. Crackin Good Bakers, Inc.*, 777 F.2d 1497 (11th Cir. 1985) (similar rule); *McKinney v. Dole*, 765 F.2d 1129 (D.C. Cir. 1985) (similar rule); *Delgado v. Lehman*, 43 F.E.P. Cases. 593 (E.D. Va. 1987) (employer treated men and women differently by maintaining hostile work environment).

c. Evidence of "harm"

(1) Proving "quid pro quo" sexual harassment.

To prove a quid pro quo sexual harassment case, the plaintiff must prove:

a) that the employee was a member of a protected class;

b) that the employee was subjected to unwelcome conduct, *see* a. "Unwelcomeness" above;

c) that the harassment complained of was based upon the sex of the plaintiff (i.e. conduct involved sexual advances or requests for sexual favors or other verbal or physical conduct of a sexual nature, *see* b. "Sexual Advances, etc." above);

d) that the employee's submission to the unwelcome conduct was an express or implied condition for receiving job benefits or that the employee's refusal to submit to the harassing demands resulted in a tangible job detriment; and

e) the harassment was carried out by a Title VII "employer" or "agent" of that employer. *Sparks v. Pilot Freight Carriers,* 830F.2d 1554 (11th Cir. 1987) (institutional employer and individual agent directly liable for own acts as those of "employer.") *See also Meritor Savings Bank v. Vinson,* 477 U.S. 57 (1986); *Huddleston v. Roger Dean Chevrolet* 845 F.2d 900 (11th Cir. 1988). Commonly referred to as *"respondeat superior," see, e.g., Henson v. City of Dundee,* 682 F.2d 897, 908 (11th Cir. 1982), but be careful about that term because it implies avoidance of liability in state tort law. In a quid pro quo claim, an employer is strictly liable for the acts of a supervisor because the supervisor relied upon his agency status to coerce the victim. *See, e.g.,* RESTATEMENT (SECOND) OF AGENCY 219(2)(d) (1958) (an agent's actions are within the scope of his employment when he acts with the apparent authority of the employer.) Thus, in quid pro quo, an employer is strictly liable where a supervisor conditions tangible job benefits upon acceptance of sexual advances (or harassing conduct). *See also Schroeder v. Schock,* 42 F.E.P. Cases 1112, 1114 (D.C. Kan. 1986).

(2) Proving "hostile work environment." To prove a hostile work environment case, the plaintiff must prove:

a) plaintiff is member of protected class;

b) plaintiff was subject to sexual harassment in form of "unwelcome" sexual or sex-based conduct in the workplace, *see* a. "Unwelcomeness" above;

c) the conduct complained of was sex-based, *see* b. "Sexual Advances, etc." above;

d) the harassment explicitly altered the terms or conditions of employment based upon sex, *e.g., Carroll v. Talman Savings & Loan Association, supra* at **a(2)** (placing specific burdens on women not placed on men) *or* was sufficiently severe or pervasive to have the purpose or effect of unreasonably interfering with the employee's job performance, *or* created an environment that is intimidating, hostile or offensive, *see, e.g., Meritor Savings Bank v. Vinson*, 477 U.S. 57 (1986); *Henson v. City of Dundee*, 682 F.2d at 903–05.

There is a battle raging around this element. The battle stems from the language, in *Henson*, 682 F.2d at 904, *Meritor Savings v. Vinson*, 477 U.S. at 57, and other cases, that environment claims could be sustained if the conditions complained of were sufficiently "severe or pervasive so as to affect seriously the psychological well-being of employees."

The best interpretation of this requirement is an objective standard that the *defendant's conduct* (or harassing agent's conduct) would affect the *reasonable person in the same circumstances*. It is critical to emphasize that the reasonable person in this instance is a female person. All the cases and the EEOC guidelines point to the *"totality of the circumstances."* Recent examples of cases searching for objective standard of reasonable person in the circumstances, see *Ross v. Double Diamond*, 45 F.E.P. Cases 317 (N.D. Tex. 1988), and *Pease v. Alford Photo*, 667 F. Supp. 1188 (W.D. Tenn. 1987) (several incidents over 2–3 months plus proof from others where sexual harassment denied by perpetrator).

Plaintiff's counsel should establish everything about the conduct and the circumstances from the complainant's point of view that would make the experience demeaning or humiliating or frightening or stressful, etc. This is essential to prove that a reasonable female person would be under stress. This is an inherently fact-based inquiry and skill is required to draw these facts out. All incidents need not be directed at the plaintiff as some defendants attempt to argue. *See, e.g., Walker v. Ford Motor Co.; Rogers v. EEOC,* 454 F.2d 234 (5th Cir. 1971), *cert. denied,* 406 U.S. 957 (1972) (EEOC subpoena for information concerning segregation of clients as support for discrimination claim of employees); *Barbetta v. Chemlawn Services Corp.* 44 F.E.P. Cases 1563 (W.D. NY 1987) (presence of pictures alone sufficient to meet summary judgment); *Broderick v. Ruder,* 685 F. Supp. 1269 (D.D.C. 1988) (defendant maintained discriminatory work environment *vis-a-vis* plaintiff by, *inter alia,* permitting supervisors to give raises and promotions to other women in the workplace based on sexual favors).

There is a minimum threshold such that one or two racist or sexist comments will not sustain a claim unless the conduct is really outrageous. *See Porta v. Rollins Environmental Services, Inc.,* 645 F.Supp. 1275 (D.C.N.J. 1987) (summary judgment in sex case); *Volk v. Coler,* 638 F.Supp. 1555 (C.D.Ill. 1986); *Vaughn v. Pool Offshore Co.,* 29 F.E.P. Cases 1017 (5th Cir. 1982) (race case; comments where complainant joined in do not make a case); *Cariddi v. Kansas Chiefs Football Club, Inc.,* 568 F.2d 87, 88 (8th Cir. 1977) (race case; a few sporadic comments do not make a case). Some courts have made bad calls, however, and discounted severe mistreatment.

Where an institutional employer was alert to potential problems and acted *quickly and surely* to put a stop to bad conduct, the claim may not be sufficiently "severe" or "pervasive" with respect to liability of an "employer" who was not the bad actor. So far, however, the courts are setting a high standard for "prompt and effective remedial action." *See Bennett v. Corroon & Black Corp.,* 845 F.2d 104 (5th Cir. 1988), *cert. denied,* 109 S.Ct. 1140 (1989). *Tunis v. Corning Glass Works,* 698 F.Supp. 452 (S.D.N.Y.

1988); *Llewellyn v. Celanese Corp.*, 693 F.Supp. 369 (W.D.N.C. 1988).

Watch out! Defendants may argue that plaintiff must prove *both* creation of an intimidating, hostile or offensive working environment *and* that the environment in fact interfered with the plaintiff's work performance or in fact did seriously affect the plaintiff's psychological well-being (not just the likelihood of such affect); there is at least dicta supporting such an argument. *See, e.e., Rabidue v. Osceola Refining Co.*, 805 F.2d 611, 619 (6th Cir. 1986), *cert. denied*, 107 S.Ct. 1983 (1987). This is a significant increase in the standard of proof. Resist this tendency by reading the original language of the EEOC Guidelines closely and using cases that follow the original language of the Guidelines and of *Rogers, Henson, Vinson* and others. *See also* discovery and evidentiary issues below.

Moreover, some courts, like the *Rabidue* court, discount sex-based hostile environment claims as being *de minimis* and business as usual, particularly in employment settings where women were previously excluded, something a reasonable person would expect. This position will probably meet with disapproval because it contradicts the basic public policy of Title VII. *See, Meritor Savings Bank v. Vinson*, 477 U.S. 57, 64 (1986), *quoting Sprogis v. United Air Lines, Inc*, 444 F.2d 1194 1198 (7th Cir 1971). Some circuits are already squarely rejecting the *Rabidue* approach *See Lipsett v. University of Puerto Rico*, 864 F.2d 881 (1st Cir. 1988); *Davis v. Monsanto Chemical Co.*, 858 F. 2d 345 (6th Cir. 1988) (race case). It is wise to rely also upon race cases for support to rebut this argument. *See, e.g., Snell v. Suffolk County*, 782 F.2d 1094 (2d Cir. 1986) (racial harassment); *Walker v. Ford Motor Co.*, 684 F.2d 1355 (11th Cir. 1982) (racial harassment). *See also Cummings v. Walsh Construction Co.*, 561 F. Supp. 872, 878 (S.D. Ga. 1983) (rejecting defendant's motion to dismiss sexual harassment suit in construction). *Meritor Savings Bank* provides solid support for evaluating race and sex hostile environment cases the same.

d. "Employer" responsibility, agency, "respondeat superior," constructive knowledge, etc.

If the perpetrator is an "employer" by definition, the employer will be liable. If the employer knew or should have known of the harassment and failed to take prompt remedial action ("condonation and ratification"), the employer will be liable. Knowledge may be "actual," by proof of appropriate agents present to observe or by notice provided by victim, or "constructive" by proof that the harassment was sufficiently pervasive to lead to the conclusion that the employer "should have known." *See, e.g., Meritor Savings Bank v. Vinson,* 477 U.S. 57 (1986) (absence of actual notice not fatal); *Yates v. Avco Corp.,* 819 F.2d 630, 636 (6th Cir. 1987) (employer should have discovered supervisor work environment harassment); *Bohen v. City of East Chicago,* 799 F.2d 1180, 1189 (7th Cir. 1986) (employer "knew the general picture if not the details" of harassment); *Katz v. Dole,* 709 F.2d 251, 255 (4th Cir. 1983) (stating general rule); *Henson v. City of Dundee,* 682 F.2d 897, 910 (11th Cir. 1982) (stating general rule).

Proving "constructive discharge" because of sexual harassment. Unless she was expressly fired, non-promoted, demoted, etc. in connection with or as a result of the sexual harassment, the plaintiff may have no monetary relief claims unless she can prove "constructive discharge," i.e. that the mistreatment or hostile conditions were so bad that she was effectively discharged. (Note however that Civil Rights Act of 1990 would add compensatory and punitive damages for the duress to Title VII; in addition pendent state claims based on state, county or local discrimination laws or state personal injury claims might afford an opportunity for compensatory and punitive damages). The standard for constructive discharge may apply whether she left work as a result of the discrimination either permanently or temporarily. Many women do reasonably feel compelled to stay away from work because of harassment. *See,* for example, results of the U.S. Merit Systems Protection Board study, *Sexual Harassment in the Federal Government: An Update* (1988). The legal standard is whether "the employer deliberately makes an employee's working conditions so intolerable that the employee is forced into involuntary resignation," *Bourque v. Powell Electrical Mfg. Co,* 617 F.2d 61, 65 (5th Cir. 1980) citing *Young v. South Western Savings & Loan Assn.,* 509 F.2d 140, 143 (5th Cir. 1975). The imposition of intolerable working conditions need not be with the purpose of forcing the employee to resign. *Id.* citing *e.g. Muller v. United States Steel Corp.,* 509 F.2d 923, 929 (10th Cir.) *cert. denied,* 423 U.S. 825 (1975). *Bourque* rejects such a rule as "inconsistent . . . with the realities of modern employment" and instead applies a standard that the "trier of fact must be satisfied that the . . . working conditions would have been so difficult or unpleasant that a reasonable person in the employee's shoes would have felt compelled to resign." *Id.* citing *Alicia Rosado v. Garcia Santiago,* 562 F.2d 114, 119 (1st Cir. 1977). It should therefore be "sufficient if the employer simply tolerates discriminatory working conditions that would drive a reasonable person to resign." *Hopkins v. Price Waterhouse,* 825 F.2d 458, 472 (D.C. Cir. 1987), *aff'd,* 109 S. Ct. 1775 (1989). Helpful sexual harassment cases include: *Huddleston v. Roger Dean Chevrolet, Inc.,* 845 F.2d 900, 905 (11th Cir. 1988) ("If the intolerable working conditions are the result of a hostile environment caused by sexual harassment, then the constructive discharge violates Title VII."); *Brooms v. Regal Tube Co.,* 44 F.E.P. Cases 1119 (N.D. Ill. 1987) (Workplace conditions intolerable and "poisoned," same standard for both). *But see, Yates v. Avco Corp.,* 819 F. 2d 630, 637 (6th Cir. 1987) (no constructive discharge where plaintiff, after her reassignment, left work due to chance encounter with former harassing supervisor and did not allow defendant to explain that former supervisor would not work in proximity to plaintiff's new position); *Carrero v. New York City Housing Authority,* 680 F. Supp. 87 (S.D.N.Y. 1987) (harassment found but "back pay" denied for period in which plaintiff chose not to work at lower status job with same employer). Proving constructive discharge during temporary and permanent absences from work can be very difficult. One theme in the cases is that it is best to attack discrimination within the context of existing employment relations, *see Hopkins v Price Waterhouse,* 825 F.2d 458, 473 (D.C. 1987), *aff'd,* 109 S.Ct. 1775 (1989); *Bourque,* 617 F.2d at 66. It may be useful to cite this theme in plaintiff's favor where she has not resigned but has many absences from work.

2. Who may be a plaintiff under Title VII?

Any "employee" of an employer in interstate commerce having 15 or more employees, etc., or of a city, state or federal government employer except the non-civilian aspect of the military, 42 U.S.C. 2000e, who is a victim of sexual harassment.

a. "Third party beneficiary" plaintiff and nepotism.

The EEOC Guidelines on Sexual Harassment, 29 C.F.R. 1611.4(h), contemplate that those passed over due to sexual favoritism would have a claim of discrimination. *See King v. Palmer,* 778 F.2d 878, 880, (D.C. Cir. 1985); *Priest v. Rotary,* 634 F. Supp. 571, 581 (N.D. Cal. 1986); *Toscano v. Nimmo,* 570 F. Supp. 1197, 1199 (D.Del. 1983). *But see DeCintio v. Westchester County Medical Center,* 807 F.2d 304 (2d Cir. 1986) (claim by males that their employment status was hurt by sexual favoritism to females not cognizable). Resist any tendency to use this concern as a basis for nepotism policies that exclude related persons from the workplace because such nepotism rules can have a disparate impact on women. Nepotism problems can be better handled by acknowledgment of the existence of relationships and rules restricting opportunity to use power of personal liaisons to affect employment opportunities. *See* BNA Special Report, Corporate Affairs: Nepotism, Office Romance and Sexual Harassment (1988).

b. The so-called "bi-sexual supervisor" defense.

Some defendants still claim that sexual harassment is not sex-based if the supervisor is bisexual because members of both sexes can be harassed, *see, e.g., Barnes v. Castle,* 561 F.2d 983 (D.C. Cir. 1977). ("bisexual defense"). Title VII protects "any individual" from employment related discrimination "based upon sex." So, for example, if a supervisor conditions a woman's job status on grant of sexual favors on day one and then does the same to a man's job status on day two, the one discriminatory act does not cancel out the other. On the other hand, if the environment is equally bad for both sexes that may not be discrimination unless the treatment can be shown to be "based upon [the] sex" of the individual. Generally, a close examination of the facts reveals that there is a differ-

141

ent level of harassment or that it is more burdensome to women (for example because they are in the extreme minority). Women are statistically more often the victims of sexual harassment and of more severe harassment. *See, e.g.,* U.S. Merit Systems Protection Board, *Sexual Harassment in the Federal Workplace* (1981).

3. Liability of an alleged defendant and who may be a defendant under Title VII?

A government employer (not including military) 42 U.S.C. 2000e-16 or an employer in interstate commerce having 15 or more employees working 20 weeks or more, 42 U.S.C. 2000e (b)— and/or "any agent" of such employer, *id.* (Unions and job referral agencies are also covered under Title VII.) Courts have held that supervisory employees can be "agents" of the employer and thus defendants in the suit. Some argue that this applies only if that supervisor has harassed the employee. Others argue that knowledge of the harassment and failure to take steps to prevent it ("ratification and condonation") where a supervisor had the power to do so is sufficient basis for "agent of employer" liability. It seems fairly clear that an institutional and an individual supervisor are both liable for that individual supervisor's harassing acts where he harassed someone with whom he had a supervisory relationship. *See, e.g., Yates v. Avco Corporation,* 819 F.2d 630 (6th Cir. 1987). It is also fairly clear that an institutional employer is liable for acts of supervisors out of line authority and/or of coworkers where the institution, through its agents, knew or should have known of the harassment and failed to take meaningful steps to stop it (ratification and condonation). Because employer "knowledge" is a key element in such suits, it is desirable, as a litigating safeguard, for the employee where possible to give written notice of the basic problems of which she complains; however, such notice is not a requirement and often practical considerations may weigh persuasively into a decision not to resort to the formality of written notice. The concept of "apparent authority" may be available to support a claim against an institutional employer on the grounds that a supervisor, co-worker or other "agent" who did not have actual agency power to affect an employee's employment status nonetheless acted with apparent authority. *Cf. ASME v. Hydrolevel,* 456

U.S. 556 (1982). *Meritor Savings Bank v. Vinson* confirmed that failure of the employee to formally notify the company or to go through internal (as contrasted to law-mandated EEO administrative procedures) does not preclude suit. The questions would be factual whether company procedures alleged as any defense reasonably could have resolved the problem where an employee failed to avail herself of procedures.

4. Jurisdictional/procedural prerequisites to Title VII suit.

Note that the administrative procedural timelines probably *do not* toll the statute of limitations for any related claims based on any legal ground other than Title VII.

a. Administrative complaint prerequisite/stringent time deadlines

CAUTION: REVIEW THESE DEADLINES BY REFERENCE TO THE STATUTES AND REGULATIONS EACH AND EVERY TIME YOU COUNSEL A POTENTIAL CLIENT. Complainant must file an administrative complaint with the appropriate federal and local/state equal employment enforcement agency within a specified time period following the last discriminatory act. Federal employees must file with the designated EEO contact within 30 days! (Note Civil Rights Act of 1990 changes period to 90 days.) Employees of private employers and of state and local government employers must file with the federal Equal Employment Opportunity Commission within 180 days unless there is a state deferral agency with which a charge is filed as well in which case the period is extended to 300 days. Practice tip: To ensure that you can sue individuals as defendants in court name them in the administrative complaint. Naming is probably not a jurisdictional prerequisite, only a condition precedent; split in circuits. Also try at least generally to characterize the discrimination broadly to avoid any successful claim that "she did not complain about *that* to the EEOC."

b. Deadline for filing in court

The administrative procedure will result in a "Notice of Right To Sue" letter to the complainant. Upon *receipt* of that notice the complainant has ninety (90) days within which to file in federal court. A party who wishes to go to court quickly may request a "Notice of Right To Sue" without waiting for an administrative determination in certain circumstances.

c. Pleading requirements

Federal courts require the plaintiff to plead that she has satisfied the prerequisites (namely administrative complaint filing and timely court filing) in the complaint and have been known to dismiss a complaint (usually without prejudice) for failure of this condition.

5. Title VII Remedies

Title VII remedies include declaratory and injunctive relief, back pay, front pay under certain conditions, *see Arnold v. City of Seminole,* 614 F.Supp. 853 (E.D. Okla 1985), attorney's fees and costs. No compensatory or punitive damages.*

B. Other Potential Legal Bases for Discrimination Claims (this is to inspire thinking, it is not comprehensive).

1. Federal and state equal protection or due process clauses and state equal rights amendments.

2. 42 U.S.C. 1983 and related civil rights where state government is employer. *See Bohen v. East Chicago,* 799 F.2d 1180 (7th Cir. 1986), but check as the status of the Civil Rights Laws of 1866 are in flux. Also it is not permissible to use the 1866 statutes to bypass Title VII procedural requirements under 1985 at least. *See Great American Savings and Loan Assn. v. Novotny,* 442 U.S. 366 (1979). May provide damages.

3. State and local equal employment, human rights and public accommodations laws. These may reach smaller employers and may also afford compensatory and punitive damages, not available under Title VII. But watch election of forum which may be claim preclusive. *Kremer v. Chemical Construction Corp.,* 456 U.S. 461 (1981).

* Limited compensatory damages are now available as a result of the Civil Rights Act of 1991.

144

4. Title IX of the Education Amendments of 1972, as amended by the Civil Rights Restoration Act, may provide a basis for *damages* where "intentional" discrimination is shown. Remember to refer complaint to the Office of Civil Rights for the Department of Education to avoid an administrative exhaustion bar.

5. Executive Order 11246. Particularly for federal contractors. Contact the Office for Federal Contract Compliance Programs of the Department of Labor.

6. Common Law Claims and Defenses   a. In sexual harassment contexts, plaintiffs have sustained claims for damages upon common law tort claims, such as assault, battery, and intentional infliction of emotional distress, interference with contract. *See, e.g., Pease v. Alford Photo Industries, Inc.,* 667 F.Supp. 1188, 1190 (W.D. Tenn. 1987) (pendent state claim) (unwelcome "sexually harassing and humiliating touching" by president of company constituted assault, battery, invasion of privacy, and intentional infliction of emotional distress so that company and president jointly and severally liable for $2,500 in compensatory and $10,000 in punitive damages); *Clark v. World Airways,* 24 F.E.P. Cases 305, 310 (D.D.C. 1980) (upholding jury verdict of $52,500 in punitive damages against employer for assault and battery); *Ford v. Revlon, Inc.,* 43 F.E.P. Cases 213 (Arizona Sup. Ct. 1987) (corporation held independently liable for intentional infliction of emotional distress when harasser (individual) found not liable. Failure to take action was itself outrageous where harassment was reported and observed.); *O'Reilly v. Executone of Albany, Inc.,* 121 A.D.2d 772, 503 N.Y.S.2d 185 (3d Dept. 1986) (allegations of sexual harassment, including touching in a sexual manner, stated a cause of action for battery and intentional infliction of emotional distress against employer and supervisors); *Kyriazi v. Western Electric Co.,* 476 F.Supp. 335 (D.N.J. 1979) ($1,500 in punitive damages assessed against each of plaintiff's former supervisors for tortious interference with contract); *But see Studstill v. Borg Warner Leasing,* 806 F.2d 1005 (11th Cir. 1986) (verbal sexual harassment did not constitute act sufficiently heinous to support claim for inten-

tional infliction of emotional distress) (applying Florida law); *Miller v. Aluminum Company of America,* 45 F.E.P. Cases 1775 (W.D. Pa. 1988) (an embarrassing remark about plaintiff's breasts, does not amount to "outrageous" behavior sufficient to support tort claim); *Belanoff v. Grayson,* 98 A.D.2d 353, 471 N.Y.S.2d 91 (supervisor's allegedly unjustified unfavorable performance evaluation and work-related criticism does not constitute intentional infliction of emotional distress, which requires a "deliberate and malicious campaign . . . exceed[ing] all bounds usually tolerated by society"). Watch statute of limitations which vary from state to state—intentional torts often limited to 1 year from date of occurrences.

b. Affirmative Defense to Common Law Claim: State Workmen's Compensation Laws.

Depending upon state law, an institutional employer but not an individual harasser may assert an affirmative defense that common law claims are precluded by workmen's compensation laws. The state decisions are split on the question whether workmen's compensation bars damages for sexual harassment. *See, generally* 2A Larson, *The Law of Workmen's Compensation* 368.30 13–40 (1983) (non-physical not covered).

II. DISCOVERY AND EVIDENTIARY PROBLEMS

A. Victim's own sexual activity and sex-related conduct should not be generally discoverable; however, if limited to workplace, conduct may be discoverable if there is some theory of relevance.

1. The victim's sex-related conduct in the workplace could be discoverable, if it goes to the issue of whether the harasser's advances were unwelcome. *Meritor Savings Bank,* 477 U.S. at 69, 106 S. Ct. at 2407 (complainant's sexually provocative speech or dress may be relevant and not per se inadmissible). *But see, Mitchell v. Hutchings,* 44 F.E.P. Cases 615, 617–18 (D. Utah 1987) (no discovery of victim's work place conduct because not alleged to have been already

known by and therefore had no bearing on what harasser thought was unwelcome; as to emotional distress claim, discovery of general atmosphere involving sexual behavior in workplace, whether or not known to defendants, permitted as relevant to whether defendants' behavior violated accepted standards of decency and morality).

2. Information as to plaintiff's sexual history and off-work conduct is not discoverable.

Mitchell v. Hutchings, 44 F.E.P. Cases 615, 618 (D. Utah 1987) (sexual promiscuity outside workplace not relevant to damages); *Priest v. Rotary,* 98 F.R.D. 755 (N.D. Cal. 1983) (notwithstanding contention that plaintiff was "sexually aggressor in [the] relationship," detailed information of plaintiff's prior sexual relations not discoverable as to character, habit or motive and because of likely chilling effect of such discovery upon sexual harassment claims worthy of protective order); *Vinson v. Superior Court of Alameda Country,* 43 Cal. 3d 833, 239 Cal. Rptr. 292, 740 P.2d 404, 411 (1987) (plaintiff's sexual history and practices not relevant to claim for emotional distress because there was no allegation that harassment impaired victim's sexuality).

B. Mental examination and psychological history of the plaintiff not obtainable, unless plaintiff has put her mental condition "in controversy" *see* Fed. R. Civ. P. 35, and *then only* with close adherence to Rule 35 requirements ("good cause shown", specifics of "time, place, and manner, conditions and scope of the examination", etc.). Examination must be specifically related to harm claimed. *See generally, Schlagenhauf v. Holder,* 379 U.S. 104, 118 (1964); *see also In re Mitchell,* 563 F.2d 143 (5th Cir. 1977) (Rule 35 order requires greater showing than Rule 26).

1. Such discovery may not be obtainable in a Title VII sex harassment case that does not also involve a cause of action for damages under tort or other similar damages claim.

Robinson v. Jacksonville Shipyards, Inc., 118 F.R.D. 525 (M.D.

Fla. 1988) (in hostile environment case, plaintiff's mental condition not in controversy because liability and back pay entitlement predicated on objective standard); *but see Vermett v. Hough*, 627 F. Supp. 587, 600–01 (W.D. Mich. 1986) (court finding for employer, in part, because plaintiff's journal and defendant's psychiatric expert testimony showed plaintiff to be a woman "predisposed to interpret her experiences [as] sexual harassment"); *Collins v. Pfizer, Inc.*, 39 F.E.P. Cases 1316, 1332 (D.Conn. 1985) (testimony of plaintiff's psychologist and evidence of past psychiatric problems and involvement in prior sexual harassment suit causes court "considerable hesitation" in accepting plaintiff's testimony and is factor in denial of claim).

2. However, where plaintiff seeks damages for emotional distress, her mental condition may be "in controversy" and such discovery has been allowed. *Compare Cody v. Marriott Corp.*, 103 F.R.D. 421 (D. Mass. 1984) (in sexual harassment case for physical damages and emotional distress but not psychiatric injuries, court refused order of mental examination because it would produce undesirable result of routinely ordering mental examination whenever a claim of damages for emotional distress was presented) *with Lowe v. Philadelphia Newspapers, Inc.*, 101 F.R.D. 296, 298–99 (E.D. Pa. 1983) (deposition of plaintiff's treating psychiatrist and examination by defendant's psychiatric expert); *Ryzlak v. McNeil Pharmacy Co.*, 38 Fed. R. Serv. 2d 443, 444 (E.D. Pa. 1982) (defendant entitled to two 90-minute psychological examinations); *Vinson v. Superior Court of Alameda County*, 43 Ca. 3d 833, 840–41, 239 Cal. Rptr. 292, 298–300, 740 P.2d 404, 410–12 (1987) (mental examinations ordered). *see also Broderick v. Shad*, 117 F.R.D. 306, 309 (D.D.C. 1987) (denying employer access to plaintiff's medical records, but only on her sworn statement that she did not seek medical treatment for "severe psychological stress" alleged in complaint).

NOTE: Depending on state law, allegations of mental or physical injury may waive physician/client or psychiatrist/client privilege. Consider carefully impact on client.

3. Techniques to prevent abuse are frequently ordered by the court.
Zabkowicz v. West Bend Co., 585 F. Supp. 635 (E.D. Wis. 1984), *aff'd in relevant part,* 789 F.2d 540 (7th Cir. 1986) (plaintiffs entitled, at their option, to presence of third party, including counsel, or a recording device, notwithstanding that this may inhibit psychiatric interview); *Lowe v. Philadelphia Newspapers, Inc.,* 101 F.R.D. 296, 299 (plaintiff's medical expert may be present but solely as observer; plaintiff's counsel excluded).

C. Incidents of other discriminatory conduct, such as sexual harassment by or of other employees to show pattern of discrimination or employer knowledge may be subject to discovery greater than typically permitted in a non-sexual harassment case.

Yates v. Avco Corp., supra, 819 F.2d at 634–36 (evidence of other harassing acts by supervisor relevant in determining constructive notice to employer); *Vinson v. Taylor,* 753 F.2d 141 (D.C. Cir) *reh. & reh. en banc denied,* 760 F.2d 1330 (D.C. Cir. 1985), *aff. on other issues raised in petition for cert. sub nom. Meritor Savings Bank v. Vinson,* 477 U.S. 57 (1986) (exclusion of evidence of Taylor's sexual harassment of other female employees is reversible error); *Delgado v. Lehman,* 665 F. Supp. 460 (E.D. Va. 1987). *But see Jones v. Flagship International,* 793 F.2d 714, 721 n.7 (5th Cir. 1986), *cert. denied,* 107 S. Ct. 952 (1987) (sexually harassing incidents of other female employees not relevant to individual claim, absent evidence that such incidents affected plaintiff's wellbeing.)

USEFUL SOURCES:

BNA   Personnel Politics Forum Survey No. 144, Sexual Harassment: Employer Policies and Problems (June 1987) (survey of corporate employment programs and policies on sexual harassment; good resource remedies).

U.S. Merit Systems Protection Board, *Sexual Harassment in the Federal Government: An Update* (1988) and *Sexual Harassment in the Federal Workplace* (1981) (surveys of incidence of sexual harassment).

NOW LDEF Video and Video Guide: "Walking the Corporate Fine Line: Sexual Harassment." (1988)

Brief of Amici Curiae Working Women's Institute in Support of Respondent in *Meritor Savings Bank v. Vinson,* U.S. Supreme Court No. 84-1979 19 CIS Law Representatives: Labor Law Series 557 (1985–86 Term) (surveying literature on sexual harassment).

Crull,   The Impact of Sexual Harassment on the Job in *Sexuality in Organizations* 67 (1980) (the harm).

Crull,   The Stress Effects of Sexual Harassment on the Job, 52 Am. J. Orthopsychiatry 539 (1982).

Hamilton, The Emotional Consequences of Gender-Based Abuse in the *et al.,* Workplace: New Counseling Programs for Sex Discrimination, 6 Women and Therapy 155 (1987)

Sexual Harassment and Employment Discrimination Against Women (1987) Feminist Institute Clearinghouse, P.O. Box 30563, Bethesda, MD 20814

Taub,   Keeping Women in Their Place: Sex Stereotyping Per Se as a Form of Employment Discrimination, 21 Bost. Coll. L. Rev. 345 (1980) (good general background).

Contact for support of victims of sexual harassment and sex discrimination:

Women's Action for Good Employment Standards, facilitated by The Institute of Research on Women's Health, 1616 18th St. NW Suite 109B, Washington, D.C. 20009

NOW Legal Defense and Education Fund
GUIDELINES FOR ADVOCATES

Effective Complaint and Investigation Procedures for
Workplace Sexual Harassment
November 1991

What Is Sexual Harassment?

Sexual harassment is experienced by millions of women in this country. While some forms of it are probably not prohibited by law—cat calls and obscene leers on the street for example—sexual harassment is prohibited as a form of sex discrimination in the workplace by federal law (if your employer has more than 15 employees or is a government employer) and by the laws of many states, counties and municipalities. In addition, many state and local laws prohibit sex discrimination, including sexual harassment, in public accommodations. The legal definition of sexual harassment in employment adopted by the federal Equal Employment Opportunity Commission states that: "[u]nwelcome sexual advances, requests for sexual favors, and other verbal or physical conduct of a sexual nature constitute sexual harassment when any one of three criteria is met:

(1) Submission to such conduct is made either explicitly or implicitly a term or condition of the individual's employment.

(2) Submission to or rejection of such conduct by an individual is used as the basis for employment decisions affecting such individual.

(3) Such conduct has the purpose or effect of unreasonably interfering with an individual's work performance C.F.R. §1604.11(a).

In *Meritor Savings Bank v. Vinson,* 477 U.S. 57 (1986), the United States Supreme Court held that Title VII of the Civil Rights Act of 1964 gives "employees the right to work in an environment free from discriminatory conduct, insult and ridicule" even where tangible employment benefits like pay and promotion are not affected by the harassment.

It is important for the well-being of employee and employer alike to have clear and effective sexual harassment policies and procedures.

Why Have Sexual Harassment Policies?

1. Sexual harassment policies are preventive measures. The chances of harassment occurring are reduced when everyone is aware of the rules.

2. Reducing the incidence of harassment increases productivity since one result of harassment may be absenteeism and diminished productivity. Sexual harassment has been recognized by the American Psychiatric Association as potentially a "severe stressor." [American Psychiatric Association, Diagnostic and Statistical Manual of Mental Disorders, 11 (3d Ed. 1987) ("DSM-111-R").] Studies have revealed that about 25 percent of harassed women use leave time in order to avoid the situation. Of women who experience sexual harassment about 5 percent quit, 10 percent leave their place of employment with sexual harassment being one reason for the change in employment and 50 percent try to ignore it. Of the 50 percent who try to ignore sexual harassment, there is a 10 percent productivity drop in the work of the victim. The victim's peers' (who are often aware of the situation) productivity rate

drops 2 percent. [The 1988 *Working Woman* Sexual Harassment Survey, Klein Assoc., Inc. November 1988.]

3. Good policies encourage the harassed party to come forward and take action against the alleged harasser. This will, in turn, give management an opportunity to take prompt and effective corrective action in eradicating harassing behavior.

4. Good policies reduce the need for "self-help" measures. When harassment goes unchecked, third parties may become involved in trying to stop it through self-help schemes. This can pose risks to everyone, including physical violence as has happened in some cases. It can seriously complicate resolution of the problem. It can also add more emotional discomfort for the harassed woman. Effective, readily usable procedures and prompt action to stop harassment are the best means to avoid these problems. This is not to deny the importance of friends and family in supporting the woman as she goes through the process of trying to solve workplace sexual harassment.

All Sexual Harassment Policies and Procedures Should Include:

1. A concise written statement that provides clear definitions, covering both subtle and blatant behavior, of what exactly is prohibited. The policy should also detail what sanctions will apply for engaging in prohibited activity. A sexual harassment policy should be made stronger than what is strictly required by law. The more clearly the policy illustrates the problem, the less trouble you will have with any possible misunderstandings of the rules.

2. A choice of either formal or informal complaint procedures. The selection of either type of procedure will allow many women, who might hesitate in making a formal claim, feel comfortable in going through the process. The complaint procedures should include specifics for filing and investigating both the formal and informal complaints. The policy should also feature a list of those

trained to handle the complaints and it should include both their names and phone numbers and their responsibilities.

Note that internal complaint mechanisms cannot lawfully forestall a target of harassment from pursuing complaint procedures with local, state and federal equal employment enforcement agencies. Deadlines within which to file a complaint of discrimination do apply under federal, state and local laws; although pursuing an internal complaint grievance procedure arguably could stretch the time frames for such filing by "tolling" the deadlines, a target of harassment who may wish to pursue her legal remedies should not rely upon such tolling and delay filing with the appropriate federal, state or local agency because she may lose part or all of her legal rights and remedies if she does so.

3. Complaint procedure(s) which are clearly defined, especially the steps and timetables, the line of authority and methods of investigation.

4. A complaint procedure that allows for multiple entry points into the system (i.e. there should be more than one way to invoke the procedural process for filing a complaint). A multiple entry system allows the victim to report the problem to a manager or a responsible person outside her work unit if she so chooses. This is essential for the harassed woman whose supervisor is the harasser or who fears retaliation within her work unit as a result of reporting.

In addition, individuals having different life experiences or culturally different views may opt for different modes of complaint. For example, one woman may feel that it is comfortable and appropriate to complain to a manager in the line of authority while another, unwilling to pursue such avenues, would prefer to file a complaint with an EEO coordinator or the head of a women's committee in the organization.

5. A provision for a neutral and well-trained investigator to follow up on complaints.

6. Education and training. Training and education should be available for all managers and workers as a preventive measure to acquaint everyone with sexual harassment policies and procedures and how these are applied to real-life situations. Programs should also be used for those who were found to have violated the policies. Managers, other designated complaint receivers and investigators should receive special training in receiving and handling complaints.

7. A mechanism to review the sensitivity of the officers handling and investigating the complaints.

8. A way to "check" the workplace atmosphere. This can be done by setting up task forces and/or conducting periodic surveys.

Important Aspects of a Sexual Harassment Policy

1. Confidentiality

Confidentiality in the investigations is of the utmost importance to protect the complainant and to protect the employer.

Often, sexual harassment complaints are handled very haphazardly, leading to lack of confidentiality. Confidentiality is important because without it the "harassed woman" may become unfairly labeled a "troublemaker." **Lack of confidentiality** may lead to damaged careers/reputations and may undermine confidence and trust in the employer.

All communications about a complaint, written and oral, should be confidential. Information should be disclosed only on a need to know basis and with the understanding that the recipient has a duty to preserve confidentiality.

2. Multiple entry points

There should be several ways in which the complaint process may begin. Multiple entry contact points increase the likelihood that the harassed woman will report and the report will be received by someone having no self-interest in the matter.

3. Enforcement

Enforcement is an important element of a sexual harassment policy. A policy should **state what types of disciplinary actions will be taken** and possible penalties should include termination.

4. Neutral Complaint Receivers and Investigators Educated About Sexual Harassment and Investigation Techniques

The neutrality of the complaint receiver and investigator is extremely important, especially since these are the persons who will handle the complaint. For anyone who will conduct any part of an investigation, skill and training in handling inquiries according to professional investigatory techniques is essential. The investigator must know how to gather and preserve evidence without introducing biases into the information-gathering process. The investigator must not be accusatory in asking questions. For example, an investigator *should not* ask questions like "What were you wearing on X date?" An investigator *should* ask for the victim/harasser/witness to retell the story as (s)he remembers it because this will allow the victim/harasser/witness to be open and tell the story without having the investigator lead the conversation.

It is optimal for there to be a female investigator and a female receiver of complaints available; sometimes women feel uncomfortable talking to male investigators or complaint handlers.

All complaint receivers and investigators should be educated as to the phenomenon of sexual harassment and its stress effects. Without this training, he or she will be unlikely to understand the responses of the harassment target and, as a result, may judge her unfairly. For example, on the one hand, some women who have been sexually harassed control the distress very well for all outward appearances. The naive viewer might then wrongly conclude that the "harm" of the harassment is not great and/or the harassment "not all that bad." On the other hand, some women are severely affected in their job performances because of sexual harassment.

The untrained viewer may conclude that she is incompetent rather than severely injured in the harassment.

Investigation

All complaints should be investigated.

The investigation of a sexual harassment complaint is the most complex area in a sexual harassment policy. Good investigation technique, including effective unbiased interviewing, is important since a complaint is usually the word of the victim against the word of the alleged harasser. Corroborative evidence is desirable but it is not always necessary or possible since harassers often time an act of harassment very carefully to avoid detection (or embarrassment).

All matters of conduct should be specifically detailed stating the type (innuendos, physical assault, etc.), frequency and the dates. It is highly likely, however, that a woman complaining of harassment will not recall all incidents at first. In being motivated to complain she may have focused only upon the most recent and/or most salient or most upsetting event and not have thought through the extent to which this is part of a larger pattern of harassment. She should be encouraged to supply more information at a later date if she recalls further instances or perceives a pattern.

The investigator should find out if persons of the opposite sex of the harassed party were subjected to similar or different conduct by the harasser.

In all situations, the investigator should find out if the employer was aware of any other instances of harassment.

All investigators should be fully trained and aware of the sensitivity of the subject matter with which they are working and the importance of confidentiality and the techniques for ensuring confidentiality.

All records of the investigation procedure and the resolution should be kept in case further complaints are brought against the same harasser. Many harassers have multiple targets/victims. There should be a mechanism which uses this information to determine what type of sanction the harasser should receive if he is no longer a first time offender.

Advice to Advocates Who Are Assisting a Sexual Harassment Target

1. A sexual harassment target/victim will find it useful to keep contemporaneous notes of her experiences of harassment separate from her other personal records (such as a diary) and keep it at home. The victim should know that these notes may be discoverable (i.e., required to be turned over to the other side) if the case goes to court. The notes should detail date, time, location and conduct involved of each incident. It should describe who was involved, who may have observed and what exactly was said or done by each person. The notes should also indicate when, where and how superiors may have become aware of the harassment.

2. The sexual harassment target should get copies of her past work evaluations to show that the quality of her work was satisfactory. Having her mail a postmarked sealed copy of her work records (aside from her working copy) to herself and keeping the copy unopened for evidence is advisable. This is important since during employment actions an individual's employment records may disappear or be altered. The sealed records will provide evidence of her work records and their contents as of a certain date.

A sexual harassment policy is a preventive program. Such policies should aim not only to hold responsible those who engage in the prohibited activity but also to educate all those who work in a place of business on women's rights to non-harassment and respect.

Chapter 5

EEOC Guidelines

This document provides guidance on defining sexual harassment and establishing employer liability in light of recent cases.

Section 703(a)(1) of Title VII, 42 U.S.C. § 2000e-2(a) provides:

> It shall be an unlawful employment practice for an employer—
> . . . to fail or refuse to hire or to discharge any individual, or otherwise to discriminate against any individual with respect to his compensation, terms, conditions, or privileges of employment, because of such individual's race, color, religion, sex, or national origin[.]

In 1980 the Commission issued guidelines declaring sexual harassment a violation of Section 703 of Title VII, establishing criteria for determining when unwelcome conduct of a sexual nature constitutes sexual harassment, defining the circumstances under which an employer may be held liable, and suggesting affirmative steps an employer should take to prevent sexual harassment. *See* Section 1604.11 of the Guidelines on Discrimination Because of Sex, 29 C.F.R. § 1604.11 ("Guidelines"). The Commission has applied the Guidelines in its enforcement litigation, and many lower courts have relied on the Guidelines.

The issue of whether sexual harassment violates Title VII reached the Supreme Court in 1986 in *Meritor Savings Bank v. Vinson,* 106 S. Ct. 2399, 40 EPD ¶ 36,159 (1986). The Court affirmed the basic premises of the Guidelines as well as the Commission's definition. The purpose of this document is to provide guidance on the following issues in light of the developing law after *Vinson:*

—determining whether sexual conduct is "unwelcome";
—evaluating evidence of harassment;
—determining whether a work environment is sexually "hostile";

—holding employers liable for sexual harassment by supervisors; and
—evaluating preventive and remedial action taken in response to claims of sexual harassment.

BACKGROUND

A. Definition

Title VII does not proscribe all conduct of a sexual nature in the workplace. Thus it is crucial to clearly define sexual harassment: only unwelcome sexual conduct that is a term or condition of employment constitutes a violation. 29 C. F. R. § 1604.11(a). The EEOC's Guidelines define two types of sexual harassment: "quid pro quo" and "hostile environment." The Guidelines provide that "unwelcome" sexual conduct constitutes sexual harassment when "submission to such conduct is made either explicitly or implicitly a term or condition of an individual's employment," 29 C.F.R. § 1604.11(a)(1). Quid pro quo harassment occurs when "submission to or rejection of such conduct by an individual is used as the basis for employment decisions affecting such individual," 29 C.F.R. § 1604.11(a)(2).[1] The EEOC's Guidelines also recognize that unwelcome sexual conduct that "unreasonably interfer[es] with an individual's job performance" or creates an "intimidating, hostile, or offensive working environment" can constitute sex discrimination, even if it leads to no tangible or economic job consequences. 29 C.F.R. § 1604.11(a)(3).[2] The Supreme Court's decision in *Vinson* established that both types of sexual harassment are actionable under section 703 of Title VII of the

[1] *See, e.g., Miller v. Bank of America,* 600 F.2d 211, 20 EPD ¶ 30,086 (9th Cir. 1979) (plaintiff discharged when she refused to cooperate with her supervisor's sexual advances); *Barnes v. Costle,* 561 F.2d 983, 14 EPD ¶ 7755 (D.C. Cir. 1977) (plaintiff's job abolished after she refused to submit to her supervisor's sexual advances); *Williams v. Saxbe,* 413 F. Supp. 665, 11 EPD 10,840 (D.D.C. 1976), *rev'd and remanded on other grounds sub nom. Williams v. Bell,* 587 F.2d 1240, 17 EPD ¶ 8605 (D.C. Cir. 1978), *on remand sub nom. Williams v. Civiletti,* 487 F. Supp. 1387, 23 EPD ¶ 30,916 (D.D.C. 1980) (plaintiff reprimanded and eventually terminated for refusing to submit to her supervisor's sexual demands).

[2] *See, e.g., Katz v. Dole,* 709 F.2d 251, 32 EPD ¶ 33,639 (4th Cir. 1983) (plaintiff's workplace pervaded with sexual slur, insult, and innuendo and plaintiff subjected to verbal sexual harassment consisting of extremely vulgar and offensive sexually related epithets); *Henson v. City of Dundee,* 682 F.2d 897, 29 EPD ¶ 32,993 (11th Cir. 1982) (plaintiff's supervisor subjected her to numerous harangues of demeaning sexual inquiries and vulgarities and repeated requests that she have sexual relations with him); *Bundy v. Jackson,* 641 F.2d 934, 24 EPD ¶ 31,439 (D.C. Cir. 1981) (plaintiff subjected to sexual propositions by supervisors, and sexual intimidation was "standard operating procedure" in workplace).

Civil Rights Act of 1964, 42 U.S.C. § 2000e-2(a), as forms of sex discrimination.

Although quid pro quo and hostile environment harassment are theoretically distinct claims, the line between the two is not always clear and the two forms of harassment often occur together. For example, an employee's tangible job conditions are affected when a sexually hostile work environment results in her constructive discharge.[3] Similarly, a supervisor who makes sexual advances toward a subordinate employee may communicate an implicit threat to adversely affect her job status if she does not comply. "Hostile environment" harassment may acquire characteristics of "quid pro quo" harassment if the offending supervisor abuses his authority over employment decisions to force the victim to endure or participate in the sexual conduct. Sexual harassment may culminate in a retaliatory discharge if a victim tells the harasser or her employer she will no longer submit to the harassment, and is then fired in retaliation for this protest. Under these circumstances it would be appropriate to conclude that both harassment and retaliation in violation of section 704(a) of Title VII have occurred.

Distinguishing between the two types of harassment is necessary when determining the employer's liability (*see infra* Section D). But while categorizing sexual harassment as "quid pro quo," "hostile environment," or both is useful analytically these distinctions should not limit the Commission's investigations,[4] which generally should consider all available evidence and testimony under all possibly applicable theories.[5]

---

[3] To avoid cumbersome use of both masculine and feminine pronouns, this document will refer to harassers as males and victims as females. The Commission recognizes, however, that men may also be victims and women may also be harassers.

[4] For a description of the respective roles of the Commission and other federal agencies in investigating complaints of discrimination in the federal sector, *see* 29 C.F.R. § 1613.216.

[5] In a subsection entitled "Other related practices," the Guidelines also provide that where an employment opportunity or benefit is granted because of an individual's "submission to the employer's sexual advances or requests for sexual favors," the employer may be liable for unlawful sex discrimination against others who were qualified for but were denied the opportunity or benefit. 29 C.F.R. § 1604.11(g). The law is unsettled as to when a Title VII violation can be established in these circumstances. *See DeCintio v. Westchester County Medical Center,* 807 F.2d 304, 42 EPD ¶ 36,785 (2d Cir. 1986), *cert. denied,* 108 S. Ct. 89, 44 EPD ¶ 37,425 (1987); *King v. Palmer,* 778 F.2d 878, 39 EPD ¶ 35,808 (D.C. Cir. 1985), *decision on remand,* 641 F. Supp. 186, 40 EPD ¶ 36,245 (D.D.C. 1986); *Broderick v. Ruder,* 46 EPD ¶ 37,963 (D.D.C. 1988); *Miller v. Aluminum Co. of America,* 679 F. Supp. 495, 500–01 (W.D. Pa.), *aff'd mem.,* No. 88-3099 (3d Cir. 1988). However, the Commission recently analyzed the issues in its "Policy Guidance on Employer Liability Under Title VII for Sexual Favoritism" dated January 1990.

B. Supreme Court's Decision in Vinson

Meritor Savings Bank v. Vinson posed three questions for the Supreme Court:

(1) Does unwelcome sexual behavior that creates a hostile working environment constitute employment discrimination on the basis of sex;

(2) Can a Title VII violation be shown when the district court found that any sexual relationship that existed between the plaintiff and her supervisor was a "voluntary one"; and

(3) Is an employer strictly liable for an offensive working environment created by a supervisor's sexual advances when the employer does not know of, and could not reasonably have known of, the supervisor's misconduct.

1) **Facts**—The plaintiff had alleged that her supervisor constantly subjected her to sexual harassment both during and after business hours, on and off the employer's premises; she alleged that he forced her to have sexual intercourse with him on numerous occasions, fondled her in front of other employees, followed her into the women's restroom and exposed himself to her, and even raped her on several occasions. She alleged that she submitted for fear of jeopardizing her employment. She testified, however, that this conduct had ceased almost a year before she first complained in any way, by filing a Title VII suit; her EEOC charge was filed later *(see infra* at n.34). The supervisor and the employer denied all of her allegations and claimed they were fabricated in response to a work dispute.

2) **Lower Courts' Decisions**—After trial, the district court found the plaintiff was not the victim of sexual harassment and was not required to grant sexual favors as a condition of employment or promotion. *Vinson v. Taylor,* 22 EPD ¶ 30,708 (D.D.C. 1980). Without resolving the conflicting testimony, the district court found that if a sexual relationship had existed between plaintiff and her supervisor, it was "a voluntary one . . . having nothing to do with her continued employment." The district court nonetheless went on to hold that the employer was not liable for its supervisor's actions because it had no notice of the alleged sexual harassment; although the employer had a policy against discrimination and an internal grievance procedure, the plaintiff had never lodged a complaint.

The court of appeals reversed and remanded, holding the lower court should have considered whether the evidence established a violation under the "hostile environment" theory. *Vinson v. Taylor,* 753 F.2d 141, 36 EPD ¶ 34,949, *denial of rehearing en banc,* 760 F.2d 1330, 37 EPD ¶ 35,232 (D.C. Cir. 1985). The court ruled that a victim's "voluntary" submission to sexual advances has "no materiality whatsoever" to the proper inquiry: whether "toleration of sexual harassment [was] a condition of her employment." The court further held that an employer is absolutely liable for sexual harassment committed by a supervisory employee, regardless of whether the employer actually knew or reasonably could have known of the misconduct, or would have disapproved of and stopped the misconduct if aware of it.

3) Supreme Court's Opinion—The Supreme Court agreed that the case should be remanded for consideration under the "hostile environment" theory and held that the proper inquiry focuses on the "unwelcomeness" of the conduct rather than the "voluntariness" of the victim's participation. But the Court held that the court of appeals erred in concluding that employers are always automatically liable for sexual harassment by their supervisory employees.

a) "Hostile Environment" Violates Title VII—The Court rejected the employer's contention that Title VII prohibits only discrimination that causes "economic" or "tangible" injury: "Title VII affords employees the right to work in an environment free from discriminatory intimidation, ridicule, and insult" whether based on sex, race, religion, or national origin. 106 S. Ct. at 2405. Relying on the EEOC's Guidelines' definition of harassment,[6] the Court held that a plaintiff may establish a violation of Title VII "by proving that discrimination based on sex has created a hostile or abusive work environment." *Id.* The Court quoted the Eleventh Circuit's decision in *Henson v. City of Dundee,* 682 F.2d 897, 902, 29 EPD ¶ 32,993 (11th Cir. 1982):

> Sexual harassment which creates a hostile or offensive environment for members of one sex is every bit the arbitrary barrier to sexual equality at the workplace that racial harassment is to racial equality. Surely, a requirement that a man or woman run a gauntlet of sexual abuse in return for the privilege of being allowed to work and make a living can be as demeaning and disconcerting as the harshest of racial epithets.

[6] The Court stated that the Guidelines, " 'while not controlling upon the courts by reason of their authority, do constitute a body of experience and informed judgment to which courts and litigants may properly resort for guidance.' " *Vinson,* 106 S. Ct. at 2405 (quoting *General Electric Co. v. Gilbert,* 429 U.S. 125, 141–42, 12 EPD ¶ 11,240 (1976), quoting in turn *Skidmore v. Swift & Co.,* 323 U.S. 134 (1944)).

106 S. Ct. at 2406. The Court further held that for harassment to violate Title VII, it must be "sufficiently severe or pervasive" to alter the conditions of [the victim's] employment and create an abusive working environment.' " *Id.* (quoting *Henson,* 682 F.2d at 904).

b) **Conduct Must Be "Unwelcome"**—Citing the EEOC's Guidelines, the Court said the gravamen of a sexual harassment claim is that the alleged sexual advances were "unwelcome." 106 S. Ct. at 2406. Therefore, "the fact that sex-related conduct was 'voluntary,' in the sense that the complainant was not forced to participate against her will, is not a defense to a sexual harassment suit brought under Title VII. . . . The correct inquiry is whether [the victim] by her conduct indicated that the alleged sexual advances were unwelcome, not whether her actual participation in sexual intercourse was voluntary." *Id.* Evidence of a complainant's sexually provocative speech or dress may be relevant in determining whether she found particular advances unwelcome, but should be admitted with caution in light of the potential for unfair prejudice, the Court held.

c) **Employer Liability Established Under Agency Principles**—On the question of employer liability in "hostile environment" cases, the Court agreed with EEOC's position that agency principles should be used for guidance. While declining to issue a "definitive rule on employer liability," the Court did reject both the court of appeals' rule of automatic liability for the actions of supervisors and the employer's position that notice is always required. 106 S. Ct. at 2408–09.

The following sections of this document provide guidance on the issues addressed in *Vinson* and subsequent cases.

GUIDANCE

A. Determining Whether Sexual Conduct Is Unwelcome

Sexual harassment is "unwelcome . . . verbal or physical conduct of a sexual nature. . . ." 29 C.F.R. § 1604.11(a). Because sexual attraction may often play a role in the day-to-day social exchange between employees, "the distinction between invited, uninvited-but-welcome, offensive-but-tolerated, and flatly rejected" sexual advances may well be difficult to discern. *Barnes v. Costle,* 561 F.2d 983, 999, 14 EPD ¶ 7755 (D.C. Cir. 1977) (MacKinnon J., concurring). But this distinction is essential because sexual conduct becomes unlawful only when it is unwelcome. The Eleventh Circuit provided a general definition of "unwelcome

165

conduct" in *Henson v. City of Dundee,* 682 F.2d at 903: the challenged conduct must be unwelcome "in the sense that the employee did not solicit or incite it, and in the sense that the employee regarded the conduct as undesirable or offensive."

When confronted with conflicting evidence as to welcomeness, the Commission looks "at the record as a whole and at the totality of circumstances. . . ." 29 C.F.R. § 1604.11(b), evaluating each situation on a case-by-case basis. When there is some indication of welcomeness or when the credibility of the parties is at issue, the charging party's claim will be considerably strengthened if she made a contemporaneous complaint or protest.[7] Particularly when the alleged harasser may have some reason (e.g., a prior consensual relationship) to believe that the advances will be welcomed, it is important for the victim to communicate that the conduct is unwelcome. Generally, victims are well-advised to assert their right to a workplace free from sexual harassment. This may stop the harassment before it becomes more serious. A contemporaneous complaint or protest may also provide persuasive evidence that the sexual harassment in fact occurred as alleged *(see infra* Section B). Thus, in investigating sexual harassment charges, it is important to develop detailed evidence of the circumstances and nature of any such complaints or protests, whether to the alleged harasser, higher management, coworkers or others.[8]

While a complaint or protest is helpful to charging party's case, it is not a necessary element of the claim. Indeed, the Commission recognizes that victims may fear repercussions from complaining about the harassment and that such fear may explain a delay in opposing the conduct. If the victim failed to complain or delayed in complaining, the investigation must ascertain why. The relevance of whether the victim has complained varies depending upon "the nature of the sexual advances and the context in which the alleged incidents occurred." 29 C.F.R. § 1604.11(b).[9]

[7] For a complaint to be "contemporaneous," it should be made while the harassment is ongoing or shortly after it has ceased. For example, a victim of "hostile environment" harassment who resigns her job because working conditions have become intolerable would be considered to have made a contemporaneous complaint if she notified the employer of the harassment at the time of her departure or shortly thereafter. The employer has a duty to investigate and, if it finds the allegations true, to take remedial action including offering reinstatement *(see infra* Section E).

[8] Even when unwelcomeness is not at issue, the investigation should develop this evidence in order to aid in making credibility determinations *(see infra* p. 12).

[9] A victim of harassment need not always confront her harasser directly so long as her conduct demonstrates the harasser's behavior is unwelcome. *See, e.g., Lipsett v. University of Puerto Rico,* 864 F.2d 881, 898, 48 EPD ¶ 38,393 (1st Cir. 1988) ("In some instances a woman may have the responsibility for telling the man directly that his comment or conduct is unwelcome. In other instances, however, a woman's consistent failure to respond to

Example—Charging Party (CP) alleges that her supervisor subjected her to unwelcome sexual advances that created a hostile work environment. The investigation into her charge discloses that her supervisor began making intermittent sexual advances to her in June 1987, but she did not complain to management about the harassment. After the harassment continued and worsened, she filed a charge with EEOC in June 1988. There is no evidence CP welcomed the advances. CP states that she feared that complaining about the harassment would cause her to lose her job. She also states that she initially believed she could resolve the situation herself, but as the harassment became more frequent and severe, she said she realized that intervention by EEOC was necessary. The investigator determines CP is credible and concludes that the delay in complaining does not undercut CP's claim.

When welcomeness is at issue, the investigation should determine whether the victim's conduct is consistent, or inconsistent, with her assertion that the sexual conduct is unwelcome.[10]

In *Vinson,* the Supreme Court made clear that voluntary submission to sexual conduct will not necessarily defeat a claim of sexual harassment. The correct inquiry "is whether [the employee] *by her conduct* indicated that the alleged sexual advances were unwelcome, not whether her actual participation in sexual intercourse was voluntary." 106 S. Ct. at 2406 (emphasis added). *See also* Commission Decision No. 84-1 ("acquiescence in sexual conduct at the workplace may not mean that the conduct is welcome to the individual").

In some cases the courts and the Commission have considered

suggestive comments or gestures may be sufficient to communicate that the man's conduct is unwelcome"); Commission Decision No. 84-1, CCH EEOC Decisions ¶ 6839 (although charging parties did not confront their supervisor directly about his sexual remarks and gestures for fear of losing their jobs, evidence showing that they demonstrated through comments and actions that his conduct was unwelcome was sufficient to support a finding of harassment).

[10] Investigators and triers of fact rely on objective evidence, rather than subjective, uncommunicated feelings. For example, in *Ukarish v. Magnesium Electron,* 33 EPD ¶ 34,087 (D.N.J. 1983), the court rejected the plaintiff's claim that she was sexually harassed by her co-worker's language and gestures; although she indicated in her personal diary that she did not welcome the banter, she made no objection and indeed appeared to join in "as one of the boys." *Id.* at 32,118. In *Sardigal v. St. Louis National Stockyards Co.,* 41 EPD ¶ 36,613 (S.D. Ill. 1986), the plaintiff's allegation was found not credible because she visited her alleged harasser at the hospital and at his brother's home, and allowed him to come into her home alone at night after the alleged harassment occurred. Similarly, in the *Vinson* case, the district court noted the plaintiff had twice refused transfers to other offices located away from the alleged harasser. (In a particular charge, the significance of a charging party's refusing an offer to transfer will depend upon her reasons for doing so.)

whether the complainant welcomed the sexual conduct by acting in a sexually aggressive manner, using sexually-oriented language, or soliciting the sexual conduct. Thus, in *Gan v. Kepro Circuit Systems,* 27 EPD ¶ 32,379 (E.D. Mo. 1982), the plaintiff regularly used vulgar language, initiated sexually-oriented conversations with her co-workers, asked male employees about their marital sex lives and whether they engaged in extramarital affairs, and discussed her own sexual encounters. In rejecting the plaintiff's claim of "hostile environment" harassment, the court found that any propositions or sexual remarks by co-workers were "prompted by her own sexual aggressiveness and her own sexually-explicit conversations" *Id.* at 23,648.[11] And in *Vinson,* the Supreme Court held that testimony about the plaintiff's provocative dress and publicly expressed sexual fantasies is not *per se* inadmissible but the trial court should carefully weigh its relevance against the potential for unfair prejudice. 106 S. Ct. at 2407.

Conversely, occasional use of sexually explicit language does not necessarily negate a claim that sexual conduct was unwelcome. Although a charging party's use of sexual terms or off-color jokes may suggest that sexual comments by others in that situation were not unwelcome, more extreme and abusive or persistent comments or a physical assault will not be excused, nor would quid pro quo harassment be allowed.

Any past conduct of the charging party that is offered to show "welcomeness" must relate to the alleged harasser. In *Swentek v. USAir, Inc.,* 830 F.2d 552, 557, 44 EPD ¶ 37,457 (4th Cir. 1987), the Fourth Circuit held the district court wrongly concluded that the plaintiff's own past conduct and use of foul language showed that "she was the kind of person who could not be offended by such comments and therefore welcomed them generally," even though she had told the harasser to leave her alone. Emphasizing that the proper inquiry is "whether plaintiff welcomed the particular conduct in question from the alleged harasser," the court of appeals held that "Plaintiff's use of foul language or sexual innuendo in a consensual setting does not waive 'her legal protections against unwelcome harassment.' " 830 F.2d at 557 (quoting *Katz v. Dole,* 709 F.2d 251, 254 n.3, 32 EPD ¶ 33,639 (4th Cir. 1983)). Thus, evidence

---

[11] *See also Ferguson v. E.I. DuPont deNemours and Co.,* 560 F. Supp. 1172, 33 EPD ¶ 34,131 (D. Del. 1983) ("sexually aggressive conduct and explicit conversation on the part of the plaintiff may bar a cause of action for [hostile environment] sexual harassment"); *Reichman v. Bureau of Affirmative Action,* 536 F. Supp. 1149, 1172, 30 FEP Cases 1644 (M.D. Pa. 1982) (where plaintiff behaved "in a very flirtatious and provocative manner" around the alleged harasser, asked him to have dinner at her house on several occasions despite his repeated refusals, and continued to conduct herself in a similar manner after the alleged harassment, she could not claim the alleged harassment was unwelcome).

concerning a charging party's general character and past behavior toward others has limited, if any, probative value and does not substitute for a careful examination of her behavior toward the alleged harasser.

A more difficult situation occurs when an employee first willingly participates in conduct of a sexual nature but then ceases to participate and claims that any continued sexual conduct has created a hostile work environment. Here the employee has the burden of showing that any further sexual conduct is unwelcome, work-related harassment. The employee must clearly notify the alleged harasser that his conduct is no longer welcome.[12] If the conduct still continues, her failure to bring the matter to the attention of higher management or the EEOC is evidence, though not dispositive, that any continued conduct is, in fact, welcome or unrelated to work.[13] In any case, however, her refusal to submit to the sexual conduct cannot be the basis for denying her an employment benefit or opportunity; that would constitute a "quid pro quo" violation.

B. Evaluating Evidence of Harassment

The Commission recognizes that sexual conduct may be private and unacknowledged, with no eyewitnesses. Even sexual conduct that occurs openly in the workplace may appear to be consensual. Thus the resolution of a sexual harassment claim often depends on the credibility of the parties. The investigator should question the charging party and the alleged harasser in detail. The Commission's investigation also should search thoroughly for corroborative evidence of any nature.[14] Supervisory

[12] In Commission Decision No. 84-1, CCH Employment Practices Guide ¶ 6839, the Commission found that active participation in sexual conduct at the workplace, e.g., by "using dirty remarks and telling dirty jokes," may indicate that the sexual advances complained of were not unwelcome. Thus, the Commission found that no harassment occurred with respect to an employee who had joined in the telling of bawdy jokes and the use of vulgar language during her first two months on the job, and failed to provide subsequent notice that the conduct was no longer welcome. By actively participating in the conduct, the charging party had created the impression among her co-workers that she welcomed the sort of sexually oriented banter that she later asserted was objectionable. Simply ceasing to participate was insufficient to show the continuing activity was no longer welcome to her. *See also Loftin-Boggs v. City of Meridian,* 633 F. Supp. 1323, 41 FEP Cases 532 (S.D. Miss. 1986) (plaintiff initially participated in and initiated some of the crude language that was prevalent on the job; if she later found such conduct offensive, she should have conveyed this by her own conduct and her reaction to her co-workers' conduct).

[13] However, if the harassing supervisor engages in conduct that is sufficiently pervasive and work-related, it may place the employer on notice that the conduct constitutes harassment.

[14] As the court said in *Henson v. City of Dundee,* 682 F.2d at 912 n.25, "In a case of alleged sexual harassment which involves close questions of credibility and subjective interpretation, the existence of corroborative evidence or the lack thereof is likely to be crucial."

and managerial employees, as well as co-workers, should be asked about their knowledge of the alleged harassment.

In appropriate cases, the Commission may make a finding of harassment based solely on the credibility of the victim's allegation. As with any other charge of discrimination, a victim's account must be sufficiently detailed and internally consistent so as to be plausible, and lack of corroborative evidence where such evidence logically should exist would undermine the allegation.[15] By the same token, a general denial by the alleged harasser will carry little weight when it is contradicted by other evidence.[16]

Of course, the Commission recognizes that a charging party may not be able to identify witnesses to the alleged conduct itself. But testimony may be obtained from persons who observed the charging party's demeanor immediately after an alleged incident of harassment. Persons with whom she discussed the incident—such as co-workers, a doctor or a counselor—should be interviewed. Other employees should be asked if they noticed changes in charging party's behavior at work or in the alleged harasser's treatment of charging party. As stated earlier, a contemporaneous complaint by the victim would be persuasive evidence both that the conduct occurred and that it was unwelcome (*see supra* Section A). So too is evidence that other employees were sexually harassed by the same person.

The investigator should determine whether the employer was aware of any other instances of harassment and if so what was the response. Where appropriate the Commission will expand the case to include class claims.[17]

---

[15] In *Sardigal v. St. Louis National Stockyards Co.*, 41 EPD ¶ 36,613 at 44,694 (S.D. Ill. 1986), the plaintiff, a waitress, alleged she was harassed over a period of nine months in a restaurant at noontime, when there was a "constant flow of waitresses or customers" around the area where the offenses allegedly took place. Her allegations were not credited by the district court because no individuals came forward with testimony to support her.

It is important to explore all avenues for obtaining corroborative evidence because courts may reject harassment claims due to lack of corroborative evidence. *See Hall v. F.O. Thacker Co.*, 24 FEP Cases 1499, 1503 (N.D. Ga. 1980) (district judge did not credit plaintiff's testimony about sexual advances because it was "virtually uncorroborated"); *Neidhart v. D.H. Holmes Co.*, 21 FEP Cases 452, 457 (E.D. La. 1979), *aff'd mem.*, 624 F.2d 1097 (5th Cir. 1980) (plaintiff's account of sexual harassment rejected because "there is not a scintilla of credible evidence to corroborate [plaintiff's version]").

[16] *See* Commission Decision No. 81-17, CCH EEOC Decisions (1983) ¶ 6757 (violation of Title VII found where charging party alleged that her supervisor made repeated sexual advances toward her; although the supervisor denied the allegations, statements of other employees supported them).

[17] Class complaints in the federal sector are governed by the requirements of 29 C.F.R. § 1613 Subpart F.

Example—Charging Party (CP) alleges that her supervisor made unwelcome sexual advances toward her on frequent occasions while they were alone in his office. The supervisor denies this allegation. No one witnessed the alleged advances. CP's inability to produce eyewitnesses to the harassment does *not* defeat her claim. The resolution will depend on the credibility of her allegations versus that of her supervisor's. Corroborating, credible evidence will establish her claim. For example, three co-workers state that CP looked distraught on several occasions after leaving the supervisor's office, and that she informed them on those occasions that he had sexually propositioned and touched her. In addition, the evidence shows that CP had complained to the general manager of the office about the incidents soon after they occurred. The corroborating witness testimony and her complaint to higher management would be sufficient to establish her claim. Her allegations would be further buttressed if other employees testified that the supervisor propositioned them as well.

If the investigation exhausts all possibilities for obtaining corroborative evidence, but finds none, the Commission may make a cause finding based solely on a reasoned decision to credit the charging party's testimony.[18]

In a quid pro quo case, a finding that the employer's asserted reasons for its adverse action against the charging party are pretextual will usually establish a violation.[19] The investigation should determine the validity of the employer's reasons for the charging party's termination. If they are pretextual and if the sexual harassment occurred, then it should be inferred that the charging party was terminated for rejecting the employer's sexual advances, as she claims. Moreover, if the termination occurred because the victim complained, it would be appropriate to find, in addition, a violation of section 704(a).

C. Determining Whether a Work Environment Is "Hostile"

The Supreme Court said in *Vinson* that for sexual harassment to violate Title VII, it must be "sufficiently severe or pervasive 'to alter the conditions of [the victim's] employment and create an abusive working

[18] In Commission Decision No. 82-13, CCH EEOC Decisions (1983) ¶ 6832, the Commission stated that a "bare assertion" of sexual harassment "cannot stand without some factual support." To the extent this decision suggests a charging party can never prevail based solely on the credibility of her own testimony, that decision is overruled.
[19] *See, e.g., Bundy v. Jackson,* 641 F.2d 934, 953, 24 EPD ¶ 31,439 (D.C. Cir. 1981).

environment.' " 106 S. Ct. at 2406 (quoting *Henson v. City of Dundee,* 682 F.2d at 904. Since hostile environment harassment takes a variety of forms, many factors may affect this determination, including: (1) whether the conduct was verbal or physical, or both; (2) how frequently it was repeated; (3) whether the conduct was hostile and patently offensive; (4) whether the alleged harasser was a co-worker or a supervisor; (5) whether others joined in perpetrating the harassment; and (6) whether the harassment was directed at more than one individual.

In determining whether unwelcome sexual conduct rises to the level of a "hostile environment" in violation of Title VII, the central inquiry is whether the conduct "unreasonably interferes with an individual's work performance" or creates "an intimidating, hostile, or offensive working environment." 29 C.F.R. § 1604.11(a)(3). Thus, sexual flirtation or innuendo, even vulgar language that is trivial or merely annoying, would probably not establish a hostile environment.

1) Standard for Evaluating Harassment—In determining whether harassment is sufficiently severe or pervasive to create a hostile environment, the harasser's conduct should be evaluated from the objective standpoint of a "reasonable person." Title VII does not serve "as a vehicle for vindicating the petty slights suffered by the hypersensitive." *Zabkowicz v. West Bend Co.,* 589 F. Supp. 780, 784, 35 EPD ¶ 34,766 (E.D. Wis. 1984). *See also Ross v. Comsat,* 34 FEP cases 260, 265 (D. Md. 1984), *rev'd on other grounds,* 759 F.2d 355 (4th Cir. 1985). Thus, if the challenged conduct would not substantially affect the work environment of a reasonable person, no violation should be found.

> *Example*—Charging Party alleges that her co-worker made repeated unwelcome sexual advances toward her. An investigation discloses that the alleged "advances" consisted of invitations to join a group of employees who regularly socialized at dinner after work. The co-worker's invitations, viewed in that context and from the perspective of a reasonable person, would not have created a hostile environment and therefore did not constitute sexual harassment.

A "reasonable person" standard also should be applied to the more basic determination of whether challenged conduct is of a sexual nature. Thus, in the above example, a reasonable person would not consider the co-worker's invitations sexual in nature, and on that basis as well no violation would be found.

This objective standard should not be applied in a vacuum, however. Consideration should be given to the context in which the alleged harassment took place. As the Sixth Circuit has stated, the trier of fact must "adopt the perspective of a reasonable person's reaction to a similar environment under similar or like circumstances." *Highlander v. K.F.C. National Management Co.*, 805 F.2d 644, 650, 41 EPD ¶ 36,675 (6th Cir. 1986).[20]

The reasonable person standard should consider the victim's perspective and not stereotyped notions of acceptable behavior. For example, the Commission believes that a workplace in which sexual slurs, displays of "girlie" pictures, and other offensive conduct abound can constitute a hostile work environment even if many people deem it to be harmless or insignificant. *Cf. Rabidue v. Osceola Refining Co.*, 805 F.2d 611, 626, 41 EPD ¶ 36,643 (6th Cir. 1986) (Keith, C.J., dissenting), *cert. denied,* 107 S. Ct. 1983, 42 EPD ¶ 36,984 (1987). *Lipsett v. University of Puerto Rico,* 864 F.2d 881, 898 48 EPD ¶ 38,393 (1st Cir. 1988).

2) Isolated Instances of Harassment—Unless the conduct is quite severe, a single incident or isolated incidents of offensive sexual conduct or remarks generally do not create an abusive environment. As the Court noted in *Vinson,* "mere utterance of an ethnic or racial epithet which engenders offensive feelings in an employee would not affect the conditions of employment to a sufficiently significant degree to violate Title VII." 106 S. Ct. at 2406 (quoting *Rogers v. EEOC*, 454 F.2d. 234, 4 EPD ¶ 7597 (5th Cir. 1971), *cert. denied,* 406 U.S. 957, 4 EPD ¶ 7838 (1972)). A "hostile environment" claim generally requires a showing of a pattern of offensive conduct.[21] In contrast, in quid pro quo cases a single sexual

---

[20] In *Highlander* and also in *Rabidue v. Osceola Refining Co.*, 805 F.2d 611, 41 EPD ¶ 36,643 (6th Cir. 1986), *cert. denied,* 107 S. Ct. 1983, 42 EPD ¶ 36,984 (1987), the Sixth Circuit required an additional showing that the plaintiff suffered some degree of psychological injury. *Highlander,* 805 F.2d at 650; *Rabidue,* 805 F.2d at 620. However, it is the Commission's position that it is sufficient for the charging party to show that the harassment was unwelcome and that it would have substantially affected the work environment of a reasonable person.

[21] *See, e.g., Scott v. Sears, Roebuck and Co.,* 798 F.2d 210, 214, 41 EPD ¶ 36,439 (7th Cir. 1986) (offensive comments and conduct of co-workers were "too isolated and lacking the repetitive and debilitating effect necessary to maintain a hostile environment claim"); *Moylan v. Maries County,* 792 F.2d 746, 749, 40 EPD ¶ 36,228 (8th Cir. 1986) (single incident or isolated incidents of harassment will not be sufficient to establish a violation; the harassment must be sustained and nontrivial); *Downes v. Federal Aviation Administration,* 775 F.2d 288, 293, 38 EPD ¶ 35,590 (D.C. Cir. 1985) (Title VII does not create a claim of sexual harassment "for each and every crude joke or sexually explicit remark made on the job. . . . [A] *pattern* of offensive conduct must be proved. . . ."); *Sapp v. City of Warner-Robins,* 655 F. Supp. 1043, 43 FEP Cases 486 (M.D. Ga. 1987) (co-worker's single effort to get the plaintiff to go out with him did not create an abusive working environment); *Freedman v. American Standard,* 41 FEP Cases 471 (D.N.J. 1986) (plaintiff did not suffer a hostile environment from the receipt of an obscene message from her co-workers and a sexual solicitation from one co-worker); *Hollis v. Fleetguard, Inc.,* 44 FEP Cases 1527 (M.D. Tenn. 1987) (plaintiff's co-worker's requests, on four occasions over a four-month period,

advance may constitute harassment if it is linked to the granting or denial of employment benefits.[22]

But a single, unusually severe incident of harassment may be sufficient to constitute a Title VII violation; the more severe the harassment, the less need to show a repetitive series of incidents. This is particularly true when the harassment is physical.[23] Thus, in *Barrett v. Omaha National Bank*, 584 F. Supp. 22, 35 FEP Cases 585 (D. Neb. 1983), *aff'd*, 726 F.2d 424, 33 EPD ¶ 34,132 (8th Cir. 1984), one incident constituted actionable sexual harassment. The harasser talked to the plaintiff about sexual activities and touched her in an offensive manner while they were inside a vehicle from which she could not escape.[24]

The Commission will presume that the unwelcome, intentional touching of a charging party's intimate body areas is sufficiently offensive to alter the conditions of her working environment and constitute a violation of Title VII. More so than in the case of verbal advances or remarks, a single unwelcome physical advance can seriously poison the victim's working environment. If an employee's supervisor sexually touches that employee, the Commission normally would find a violation. In such situations, it is the employer's burden to demonstrate that the unwelcome conduct was not sufficiently severe to create a hostile work environment.

When the victim is the target of both verbal and non-intimate physical conduct, the hostility of the environment is exacerbated and a violation is more likely to be found. Similarly, incidents of sexual harassment directed at other employees in addition to the charging party are relevant to a showing of hostile work environment. *Hall v. Gus Construction Co.*, 842 F.2d 1010, 46 EPD ¶ 37,905 (8th Cir. 1988); *Hicks v. Gates Rubber Co.*, 833 F.2d 1406, 44 EPD ¶ 37,542 (10th Cir. 1987); *Jones v. Flagship*

that she have a sexual affair with him, followed by his coolness toward her and avoidance of her did not constitute a hostile environment; there was no evidence he coerced, pressured, or abused the plaintiff after she rejected his advances).

[22] *See Neville v. Taft Broadcasting Co.*, 42 FEP Cases 1314 (W.D.N.Y. 1987) (one sexual advance, rebuffed by plaintiff, may establish a prima facie case of "quid pro quo" harassment, but is not severe enough to create a hostile environment).

[23] The principles for establishing employer liability, set forth in Section D below, are to be applied to cases involving physical contact in the same manner that they are applied in other cases.

[24] *See also Gilardi v. Schroeder*, 672 F. Supp. 1043, 45 FEP Cases 283 (N.D. Ill. 1986) (plaintiff who was drugged by employer's owner and raped while unconscious, and then was terminated at insistence of owner's wife, was awarded $113,000 in damages for harassment and intentional infliction of emotional distress); Commission Decision No. 83-1, CCH EEOC Decisions (1983) ¶ 6834 (violation found where the harasser forcibly grabbed and kissed charging party while they were alone in a storeroom); Commission Decision No. 84-3, CCH Employment Practices Guide ¶ 6841 (violation found where the harasser slid his hand under the charging party's skirt and squeezed her buttocks).

International, 793 F.2d 714, 721 n.7, 40 EPD ¶ 36,392 (5th Cir. 1986), *cert. denied,* 107 S. Ct. 952, 41 EPD ¶ 36,708 (1987).

3) Non-physical Harassment—When the alleged harassment consists of verbal conduct, the investigation should ascertain the nature, frequency, context, and intended target of the remarks. Questions to be explored might include:

—Did the alleged harasser single out the charging party?

—Did the charging party participate?

—What was the relationship between the charging party and the alleged harasser(s)?

—Were the remarks hostile and derogatory?

No one factor alone determines whether particular conduct violates Title VII. As the Guidelines emphasize, the Commission will evaluate the totality of the circumstances. In general, a woman does not forfeit her right to be free from sexual harassment by choosing to work in an atmosphere that has traditionally included vulgar, anti-female language. However, in *Rabidue v. Osceola Refining Co.,* 805 F.2d 611, 41 EPD ¶ 36,643 (6th Cir. 1986), *cert. denied,* 107 S. Ct. 1983, 42 EPD ¶ 36,984 (1987), the Sixth Circuit rejected the plaintiff's claim of harassment in such a situation.[25] One of the factors the court found relevant was "the lexicon of obscenity that pervaded the environment of the workplace both before and after the plaintiff's introduction into its environs, coupled with the reasonable expectations of the plaintiff upon voluntarily entering that environment." 805 F.2d at 620. Quoting the district court, the majority noted that in some work environments, " 'humor and language are rough hewn and vulgar. Sexual jokes, sexual conversations, and girlie magazines may abound. Title VII was not meant to—or can—change this.' " *Id.* at 620–21. The court also considered the sexual remarks and poster at issue to have a "de minimis effect on the plaintiff's work environment when considered in the context of a society that condones and publicly features and commercially exploits open displays of written and pictorial

---

[25] The alleged harasser, a supervisor of another department who did not supervise plaintiff but worked with her regularly, "was an extremely vulgar and crude individual who customarily made obscene comments about women generally, and, on occasion, directed such obscenities to the plaintiff." 805 F.2d at 615. The plaintiff and other female employees were exposed daily to displays of nude or partially clad women in posters in male employees' offices. 805 F.2d at 623–24 (Keith, J., dissenting in part and concurring in part). Although the employees told management they were disturbed and offended, the employer did not reprimand the supervisor.

erotica at the newsstands, on prime-time television, at the cinema, and in other public places." *Id.* at 622.

The Commission believes these factors rarely will be relevant and agrees with the dissent in *Rabidue* that a woman does not assume the risk of harassment by voluntarily entering an abusive, anti-female environment. "Title VII's precise purpose is to prevent such behavior and attitudes from poisoning the work environment of classes protected under the Act." 805 F.2d at 626 (Keith, J., dissenting in part and concurring in part). Thus, in a decision disagreeing with *Rabidue,* a district court found that a hostile environment was established by the presence of pornographic magazines in the workplace and vulgar employee comments concerning them; offensive sexual comments made to and about plaintiff and other female employees by her supervisor; sexually oriented pictures in a company-sponsored movie and slide presentation; sexually oriented pictures and calendars in the workplace; and offensive touching of plaintiff by a co-worker. *Barbetta v. Chemlawn Services Corp.,* 669 F. Supp. 569, 45 EPD ¶ 37,568 (W.D.N.Y. 1987). The court held that the proliferation of pornography and demeaning comments, if sufficiently continuous and pervasive, "may be found to create an atmosphere in which women are viewed as men's sexual playthings rather than as their equal co-workers." *Barbetta,* 669 F. Supp. at 573. The Commission agrees that, depending on the totality of circumstances, such an atmosphere may violate Title VII. *See also Waltman v. International Paper Co.,* 875 F.2d 468, 50 EPD ¶ 39,106 (5th Cir. 1989), in which the 5th Circuit endorsed the Commission's position in its amicus brief that evidence of ongoing sexual graffiti in the workplace, not all of which was directed at the plaintiff, was relevant to her claim of harassment. *Bennett v. Corroon & Black Corp.,* 845 F.2d 104, 46 EPD ¶ 37,955 (5th Cir. 1988) (the posting of obscene cartoons in an office men's room bearing the plaintiff's name and depicting her engaged in crude and deviant sexual activities could create a hostile work environment).

4) Sex-based Harassment—Although the Guidelines specifically address conduct that is sexual in nature, the Commission notes that sex-based harassment—that is, harassment not involving sexual activity or language—may also give rise to Title VII liability (just as in the case of harassment based on race, national origin or religion) if it is "sufficiently patterned or pervasive" and directed at employees because of their sex. *Hicks v. Gates Rubber Co.,* 833 F.2d at 1416; *McKinney v. Dole,* 765 F.2d 1129, 1138, 37 EPD ¶ 35,339 (D.C. Cir. 1985).

Acts of physical aggression, intimidation, hostility or unequal treatment based on sex may be combined with incidents of sexual harassment to establish the existence of discriminatory terms and conditions of employment. *Hall v. Gus Construction Co.,* 842 F.2d at 1014; *Hicks v. Gates Rubber Co.,* 833 F.2d at 1416.

5) Constructive Discharge—Claims of hostile environment sexual harassment often are coupled with claims of constructive discharge. If constructive discharge due to a hostile environment is proven, the claim will also become one of "quid pro quo" harassment.[26] It is the position of the Commission and a majority of courts that an employer is liable for constructive discharge when it imposes intolerable working conditions in violation of Title VII when those conditions foreseeably would compel a reasonable employee to quit, whether or not the employer specifically intended to force the victim's resignation. *See Derr v. Gulf Oil Corp.,* 796 F.2d 340, 343–44, 41 EPD ¶ 36,468 (10th Cir. 1986); *Goss v. Exxon Office Systems Co.,* 747 F.2d 885, 888, 35 EPD ¶ 34,768 (3d Cir. 1984); *Nolan v. Cleland,* 686 F.2d 806, 812–15, 30 EPD ¶ 33,029 (9th Cir. 1982); *Held v. Gulf Oil Co.,* 684 F.2d 427, 432, 29 EPD ¶ 32,968 (6th Cir. 1982); *Clark v. Marsh,* 665 F.2d 1168, 1175 n.8, 26 EPD ¶ 32,082 (D.C. Cir. 1981); *Bourque v. Powell Electrical Manufacturing Co.,* 617 F.2d 61, · 65, 23 EPD ¶ 30,891 (5th Cir. 1980); Commission Decision 84-1, CCH EEOC Decision ¶ 6839. However, the Fourth Circuit requires proof that the employer imposed the intolerable conditions with the intent of forcing the victim to leave. *See EEOC v. Federal Reserve Bank of Richmond,* 698 F.2d 633, 672, 30 EPD ¶ 33,269 (4th Cir. 1983). But this case is not a sexual harassment case and the Commission believes it is distinguishable because specific intent is not as likely to be present in hostile environment cases.

An important factor to consider is whether the employer had an effective internal grievance procedure. *(See* Section E, *Preventive and Remedial Action).* The Commission argued in its *Vinson* brief that if an employee knows that effective avenues of complaint and redress are available, then the availability of such avenues itself becomes a part of the work environment and overcomes, to the degree it is effective, the hostility of the work environment. As Justice Marshall noted in his opinion in *Vinson,* "Where a complainant without good reason bypassed an internal complaint procedure she knew to be effective, a court may be reluctant to

---

[26] However, while an employee's failure to utilize effective grievance procedures will not shield an employer from liability for "quid pro quo" harassment, such failure may defeat a claim of constructive discharge. *See* discussion of impact of grievance procedures later in this section, and section D(2)(c)(2), below.

find constructive termination. . . ." 106 S. Ct. at 2411 (Marshall, J., concurring in part and dissenting in part). Similarly, the court of appeals in *Dornhecker v. Malibu Grand Prix Corp.*, 828 F.2d 307, 44 EPD ¶ 37,557 (5th Cir. 1987), held the plaintiff was not constructively discharged after an incident of harassment by a co-worker because she quit immediately, even though the employer told her she would not have to work with him again, and she did not give the employer a fair opportunity to demonstrate it could curb the harasser's conduct.

D. Employer Liability for Harassment by Supervisors

In *Vinson,* the Supreme Court agreed with the Commission's position that "Congress wanted courts to look to agency principles for guidance" in determining an employer's liability for sexual conduct by a supervisor:

> While such common-law principles may not be transferable in all their particulars to Title VII, Congress' decision to define "employer" to include any "agent" of an employer, 42 U.S.C. § 2000e(b), surely evinces an intent to place some limits on the acts of employees for which employers under Title VII are to be held responsible.

106 S. Ct. at 2408. Thus, while declining to issue a "definitive rule on employer liability," the Court did make it clear that employers are not "automatically liable" for the acts of their supervisors. For the same reason, the Court said, "absence of notice to an employer does not necessarily insulate that employer from liability." *Id.*

As the Commission argued in *Vinson,* reliance on agency principles is consistent with the Commission's Guidelines, which provide in section 1604.11(c) that:

> . . . an employer . . . is responsible for its acts and those of its agents and supervisory employees with respect to sexual harassment regardless of whether the specific acts complained of were authorized or even forbidden by the employer and regardless of whether the employer knew or should have known of their occurrence. The Commission will examine the circumstances of the particular employment relationship and the job functions performed by the individual in determining whether an individual acts in either a supervisory or agency capacity.

Citing the last sentence of this provision, the Court in *Vinson* indicated that the Guidelines further supported the application of agency principles. 106 S. Ct. at 2408.

1) Application of Agency Principles—Quid Pro Quo Cases. An employer will always be held responsible for acts of "quid pro quo" harassment. A supervisor in such circumstances has made or threatened to make a decision affecting the victim's employment status, and he therefore has exercised authority delegated to him by his employer. Although the question of employer liability for quid pro quo harassment was not at issue in *Vinson,* the Court's decision noted with apparent approval the position taken by the Commission in its brief that:

> where a supervisor exercises the authority actually delegated to him by his employer, by making or threatening to make decisions affecting the employment status of his subordinates, such actions are properly imputed to the employer whose delegation of authority empowered the supervisor to undertake them.

106 S. Ct. at 2407–08 (citing Brief for the United States and Equal Employment Opportunity Commission as *Amicus Curiae* at 22).[27] *See also Sparks v. Pilot Freight Carriers, Inc.,* 830 F.2d 1554, 44 EPD ¶ 37,493 (11th Cir. 1987) (adopting EEOC position quoted in *Vinson* opinion); *Lipsett,* 864 F.2d at 901 (adopting, for Title IX of the Education Amendments, the *Vinson* standard that an employer is absolutely liable for acts of quid pro quo harassment "whether [it]knew, should have known, or approved of the supervisor's actions"). Thus, applying agency principles, the court in *Schroeder v. Schock,* 42 FEP Cases 1112 (D. Kans. 1986), held an employer liable for quid pro quo harassment by a supervisor who had authority to recommend plaintiff's discharge. The employer maintained the supervisor's acts were beyond the scope of his employment since the sexual advances were made at a restaurant after work hours. The court held that because the supervisor was acting within the scope of

---

[27] This well-settled principle is the basis for employer liability for supervisors' discriminatory employment decisions that violate Title VII. 106 S.Ct. at 2408; *see, e.g., Anderson v. Methodist Evangelical Hospital, Inc.,* 464 F.2d 723, 725, 4 EPD ¶ 7901 (6th Cir. 1972) (racially motivated discharge "by a person in authority at a lower level of management" is attributable to employer despite upper management's "exemplary" record in race relations); *Tidwell v. American Oil Co.,* 332 F. Supp. 424, 436, 4 EPD ¶ 7544 (D. Utah 1971) (upper level management's lack of knowledge irrelevant where supervisor illegally discharged employee for refusing to disqualify black applicant discriminatorily); *Flowers v. Crouch-Walker Corp.,* 552 F.2d 1277, 1282, 14 EPD ¶ 7510 (7th Cir. 1977) ("The defendant is liable as principal for any violation of Title VII . . . by [a supervisor] in his authorized capacity as supervisor.")

his authority when making or recommending employment decisions, his conduct may fairly be imputed to the employer. The supervisor was using his authority to hire, fire, and promote to extort sexual consideration from an employee, even though the sexual advance itself occurred away from work.

2) Application of Agency Principles—Hostile Environment Cases

a) Vinson —In its *Vinson* brief the Commission argued that the employer should be liable for the creation of a hostile environment by a supervisor when the employer knew or had reason to know of the sexual misconduct. Ways by which actual or constructive knowledge could be demonstrated include: by a complaint to management or an EEOC charge; by the pervasiveness of the harassment; or by evidence the employer had "deliberately turned its back on the problem" of sexual harassment by failing to establish a policy against it and a grievance mechanism to redress it. The brief argued that an employer should be liable "if there is no reasonably available avenue by which victims of sexual harassment can make their complaints known to appropriate officials who are in a position to do something about those complaints." Brief for the United States and Equal Employment Opportunity Commission as *Amicus Curiae* at 25. Under that circumstance, an employer would be deemed to know of any harassment that occurred in its workplace.

While the *Vinson* decision quoted the Commissions's brief at length, it neither endorsed nor rejected its position.[28] 106 S. Ct. at 2407–08. The Court did state, however, that "the mere existence of a grievance procedure and a policy against discrimination, coupled with [the victim's] failure to invoke the procedure" are "plainly relevant" but "not necessarily dispositive." *Id.* at 2408–09. The Court further stated that the employer's argument that the victim's failure to complain insulated it from liability "might be substantially stronger if its procedures were better calculated to encourage victims of harassment to come forward." *Id.* at 2409.

The Commission, therefore, interprets *Vinson* to require a careful examination in "hostile environment" cases of whether the harassing supervisor was acting in an "agency capacity" (29 C.F.R. § 1604.11(c)). Whether the employer had an appropriate and effective complaint procedure and whether the victim used it are important factors to consider, as discussed below.

b) Direct Liability —The initial inquiry should be whether the employer knew or should have known of the alleged sexual harassment. If

---

[28] The Court observed that the Commission's position was "in some tension" with the first sentence of section 1604.11(c) of the Guidelines but was consistent with the final sentence of that section. (*See supra* at 21).

actual or constructive knowledge exists, and if the employer failed to take immediate and appropriate corrective action, the employer would be directly liable.[29] Most commonly an employer acquires actual knowledge through first-hand observation, by the victim's internal complaint to other supervisors or managers, or by a charge of discrimination.

An employer is liable when it "knew, or *upon reasonably diligent inquiry should have known,*" of the harassment. *Yates v. Avco Corp.,* 819 F.2d 630, 636, 43 EPD ¶ 37,086 (6th Cir. 1987) (emphasis added) (supervisor harassed two women "on a daily basis in the course of his supervision of them" and the employer's grievance procedure did not function effectively). Thus, evidence of the pervasiveness of the harassment may give rise to an inference of knowledge or establish constructive knowledge. *Henson v. City of Dundee,* 682 F.2d 897, 905, 29 EPD ¶ 32,993 (11th Cir. 1982); *Taylor v. Jones,* 653 F.2d 1193, 1197–99, 26 EPD ¶ 31,9 3 (8th Cir. 1981). Employers usually will be deemed to know of sexual harassment that is openly practiced in the workplace or well-known among employees. This often may be the case when there is more than one harasser or victim. *Lipsett,* 864 F.2d at 906 (employer liable where it should have known of concerted harassment of plaintiff and other female medical residents by more senior male residents).

The victim can of course put the employer on notice by filing a charge of discrimination. As the Commission stated in its *Vinson* brief, the filing of a charge triggers a duty to investigate and remedy any ongoing illegal activity. It is important to emphasize that an employee can always file an EEOC charge without first utilizing an internal complaint or grievance procedure[30] and may wish to pursue both avenues simultaneously because an internal grievance does not prevent the Title VII

[29] *Barrett v. Omaha National Bank,* 584 F. Supp. 22, 30–31 (D. Neb. 1983), *aff'd,* 726 F.2d 424, 33 EPD ¶ 34,132 (8th Cir. 1984); *Ferguson v. E.I. DuPont deNemours Co.,* 560 F. Supp. 1172, 1199 (D. Del. 1983); Commission Decision No. 83-1, CCH EEOC Decisions (1983) ¶ 6834. "[A]n employer who has reason to know that one of his employees is being harassed in the workplace by others on grounds of race, sex, religion, or national origin, and does nothing about it, is blameworthy." *Hunter v. Allis-Chalmers Corp.,* 797 F.2d 1417, 1422, 41 EPD ¶ 36,417 (7th Cir. 1986).

This is the theory under which employers are liable for harassment by co-workers, which was at issue in *Hunter v. Allis-Chalmers.* Section 1604.11(d) provides:

With respect to conduct between fellow employees, an employer is responsible for acts of sexual harassment in the workplace where the employer (or its agents or supervisory employees) knows or should have known of the conduct, unless it can show that it took immediate and appropriate corrective action.

Section E(2) of this paper discusses what constitutes "immediate and appropriate corrective action," and is applicable to cases of harassment by co-workers as well as supervisors.
[30] Sexual harassment claims are no different from other types of discrimination claims in this regard. *See Alexander v. Gardner-Denver Co.,* 415 U.S. 36, 52, 7 EPD ¶ 9148 (1974).

charge-filing time period from expiring.[31] Nor does the filing of an EEOC charge allow an employer to cease action on an internal grievance[32] or ignore evidence of ongoing harassment.[33] Indeed, employers should take prompt remedial action upon learning of evidence of sexual harassment (or any other form of unlawful discrimination), whether from an EEOC charge or an internal complaint. If the employer takes immediate and appropriate action to correct the harassment and prevent its recurrence, and the Commission determines that no further action is warranted, normally the Commission would administratively close the case.

c) Imputed Liability —The investigation should determine whether the alleged harassing supervisor was acting in an "agency capacity" (29 C.F.R. § 1604.11(c)).[34] This requires a determination whether the supervisor was acting within the scope of his employment (see Restatement (Second) of Agency, § 219(1) (1958)), or whether his actions can be imputed to the employer under some exception to the "scope of employment" rule (Id. at § 219(2)). The following principles should be considered, and applied where appropriate in "hostile environment" sexual harassment cases.

1. Scope of Employment—A supervisor's actions are generally viewed as being within the scope of his employment if they represent the exercise of authority actually vested in him. It will rarely be the case that an employer will have authorized a supervisor to engage in sexual harassment. See Fields v. Horizon House, Inc., No. 86-4343 (E.D. Pa. 1987) (available on Lexis, Genfed library, Dist. file). Cf. Hunter v. Allis-Chalmers Corp., 797 F.2d 1417, 1421–22, 41 EPD ¶ 36,417 (7th Cir. 1986) (co-worker racial harassment case). However, if the employer becomes aware of work-related sexual misconduct and does nothing to stop it, the

---

[31] See I.U.O.E. v. Robbins & Myers, Inc., 429 U.S. 229, 236, 12 EPD ¶ 11,256 (1976).

[32] The Commission has filed suit in such circumstances, alleging that termination of grievance processing because a charge has been filed constitutes unlawful retaliation in violation of § 704(a). See EEOC v. Board of Governors of State Colleges & Universities, 706 F. Supp. 1378, 50 EPD ¶ 39,035 (D. Ill. 1989) (denying EEOC's motion for summary judgement on ground that ADEA's retaliation provision is not violated if termination of grievance proceedings was done in good faith).

[33] See Brooms v. Regal Tube Co., 44 FEP Cases 1119 (N.D. Ill. 1987), aff'd in relevant part, 881 F.2d 412 (7th Cir. 1989).

[34] The fact that an EEOC charge puts the employer on notice of sexual harassment means that the question of imputed employer liability under agency principles often will become of secondary importance. It figured critically in the Vinson case because the plaintiff never filed an EEOC charge before filing her Title VII lawsuit. Without having given any prior notice of the sexual harassment to anyone, she waited to file her lawsuit until almost a year after she admitted it had ceased. The sexual harassment was alleged to have taken place mostly in private, and she produced no witnesses either to the alleged harassment or to its adverse effects on her. Her case did not include a constructive discharge claim, and the district court found no "quid pro quo" harassment.

employer, by acquiescing, has brought the supervisor's actions within the scope of his employment.

2. Apparent Authority—An employer is also liable for a supervisor's actions if these actions represent the exercise of authority that third parties reasonably believe him to possess by virtue of his employer's conduct. This is called "apparent authority." *See* Restatement (Second) of Agency, §§ 7,8; 219(2)(d) (1958). The Commission believes that in the absence of a strong, widely disseminated, and consistently enforced employer policy against sexual harassment, and an effective complaint procedure, employees could reasonably believe that a harassing supervisor's actions will be ignored, tolerated, or even condoned by upper management. This apparent authority of supervisors arises from their power over their employees, including the power to make or substantially influence hiring, firing, promotion and compensation decisions. A supervisor's capacity to create a hostile environment is enhanced by the degree of authority conferred on him by the employer, and he may rely upon apparent authority to force an employee to endure a harassing environment for fear of retaliation. If the employer has not provided an effective avenue to complain, then the supervisor has unchecked, final control over the victim and it is reasonable to impute his abuse of this power to the employer.[35] The Commission generally will find an employer liable for hostile environment sexual harassment by a supervisor when the employer failed to establish an explicit policy against sexual harassment and did not have a reasonably available avenue by which victims of sexual harassment could complain to someone with authority to investigate and remedy the problem. *(See* Section E.) *See also EEOC v. Hacienda Hotel,* 881 F.2d 1504, 51 EPD ¶ 39,250 (9th Cir. 1989) (finding employer liable for sexual harassment despite plaintiff's failure to pursue internal remedies where the employer's anti-discrimination policy did not specifically proscribe sexual harassment and its internal procedures required initial resort to the supervisor accused of engaging in or condoning harassment).

But an employer can divest its supervisors of this apparent authority by implementing a strong policy against sexual harassment and maintaining an effective complaint procedure. When employees know that recourse is available, they cannot reasonably believe that a harassing work environment is authorized or condoned by the employer.[36] If an em-

---

[35] *See also Fields v. Horizon House, supra* (an employer might be charged with constructive notice of a supervisor's harassment if the supervisor is vested with unbridled authority to retaliate against an employee).

[36] It is important to reemphasize, however, that no matter what the employer's policy, the employer is always liable for any supervisory actions that affect the victim's employment status, such as hiring, firing, promotion or pay. *See supra* at 21–22. Moreover, this discus-

ployee failed to use an effective, available complaint procedure, the employer may be able to prove the absence of apparent authority and thus the lack of an agency relationship, unless liability attaches under some other theory.[37] Thus, even when an employee failed to use an effective grievance procedure, the employer will be liable if it obtained notice through other means (such as the filing of a charge or by the pervasiveness of the harassment) and did not take immediate and appropriate corrective action.

> *Example*—Charging Party (CP) alleges that her supervisor made repeated sexual advances toward her that created a hostile work environment. The investigation into her charge discloses that CP had maintained an intermittent romantic relationship with the supervisor over a period of three years preceding the filing of the charge in September of 1986. CP's employer was aware of this relationship and its consensual nature. CP asserts, however, that on frequent occasions since January of 1986 she had clearly stated to the supervisor that their relationship was over and his advances were no longer welcome. The supervisor nevertheless persisted in making sexual advances toward CP, berating her for refusing to resume their sexual relationship. His conduct did not put the employer on notice that any unwelcome harassment was occuring. The employer has a well-communicated policy against sexual harassment and a complaint procedure designed to facilitate the resolution of sexual harassment complaints and ensure against retaliation. This procedure has worked well in the past. CP did not use it, however, or otherwise complain to higher management. Even if CP's allegations are true, the Commission would probably not find her employer liable for the alleged harassment since she failed to use the complaint procedure or inform higher management that the advances had become unwelcome. If CP resigned because of the alleged harassment, she would not be able to establish a constructive discharge since she failed to complain.

---

sion of apparent authority recognizes the unique nature of hostile environment sexual harassment claims and therefore is limited to such cases.

[37] *Cf. Fields v. Horizon House* ("Apparent authority is created by and flows from the acts of the principal, not from the personal beliefs of the third party."). Moreover, as noted above, an employee would find it difficult to establish a constructive discharge in this situation because she could not show she had no alternative but to resign. Failure to complain also might undermine a later assertion that the conduct occurred or was unwelcome.

In the preceding example, if the employer, upon obtaining notice of the charge, failed to take immediate and appropriate corrective action to stop any ongoing harassment, then the employer will be unable to prove that the supervisor lacked apparent authority for his conduct, and if the allegations of harassment are true, then the employer will be found liable. Or if the supervisor terminated the charging party because she refused to submit to his advances, the employer would be liable for quid pro quo harassment.

3. Other Theories—A closely related theory is agency by estoppel. *See* Restatement (Second) of Agency at § 8B. An employer is liable when he intentionally or carelessly causes an employee to mistakenly believe the supervisor is acting for the employer, or knows of the misapprehension and fails to correct it. For example, an employer who fails to respond appropriately to past known incidents of harassment would cause its employees to reasonably believe that any further incidents are authorized and will be tolerated.

Liability also may be imputed if the employer was "negligent or reckless" in supervising the alleged harasser. *See* Restatement (Second) of Agency § 219(2)(6); *Hicks v. Gates Rubber Co.,* 833 F.2d 1406, 1418, 44 EPD ¶ 37,542 (10th Cir. 1987). "Under this standard, liability would be imposed if the employer had actual or constructive knowledge of the sexual harassment but failed to take remedial action." *Fields v. Horizon House, Inc.,* No. 86-4343 (E.D. Pa. 1987). This is essentially the same as holding the employer directly liable for its failure to act.

An employer cannot avoid liability by delegating to another person a duty imposed by statute. Restatement (Second) of Agency at § 492 (1958), Introductory Note, p. 435 ("liability follows if the person to whom the performance is delegated acts improperly with respect to it"). An employer who assigns the performance of a non-delegable duty to an employee remains liable for injuries resulting from the failure of the employee to carry out that duty. Restatement, §§ 214 and 219. Title VII imposes on employers a duty to provide their employees with a workplace free of sexual harassment. An employer who entrusts that duty to an employee is liable for injuries caused by the employee's breach of the duty. *See, e.g., Brooms v. Regal Tube Co.,* 44 FEP Cases 1119 (N.D. Ill. 1987) (employer liable for sexual harassment committed by the management official to whom it had delegated the responsibility to devise and enforce its policy against sexual harassment), *aff'd on other ground,* 881 F.2d 412, 420–21 (7th Cir. 1989).

Finally, an employer also may be liable if the supervisor "was aided in accomplishing the tort by the existence of the agency relation," Restatement (Second) of Agency § 219(2)(d). *See Sparks v. Pilot Freight Carriers, Inc.,* 830 F.2d 1554, 44 EPD ¶ 37,493 (11th Cir. 1987); *Hicks v. Gates Rubber Co.,* 833 F.2d at 1418. For example, in *Sparks v. Pilot Freight Carriers,* the court found that the supervisor had used his supervisory authority to facilitate his harassment of the plaintiff by "repeatedly reminding [her] that he could fire her should she fail to comply with his advances." 830 F.2d at 1560. This case illustrates how the two types of sexual harassment can merge. When a supervisor creates a hostile environment through the aid of work-related threats or intimidation, the employer is liable under both the quid pro quo and hostile environment theories.

E. Preventive and Remedial Action

1) Preventive Action—The EEOC's Guidelines encourage employers to:

> take all steps necessary to prevent sexual harassment from occurring, such as affirmatively raising the subject, expressing strong disapproval, developing appropriate sanctions, informing employees of their right to raise and how to raise the issue of harassment under Title VII, and developing methods to sensitize all concerned.

29 C.F.R. § 1604.11(f). An effective preventive program should include an explicit policy against sexual harassment that is clearly and regularly communicated to employees and effectively implemented. The employer should affirmatively raise the subject with all supervisory and non-supervisory employees, express strong disapproval, and explain the sanctions for harassment. The employer should also have a procedure for resolving sexual harassment complaints. The procedure should be designed to "encourage victims of harassment to come forward" and should not require a victim to complain first to the offending supervisor. *See Vinson,* 106 S. Ct. at 2408. It should ensure confidentiality as much as possible and provide effective remedies, including protection of victims and witnesses against retaliation.

2) Remedial Action—Since Title VII "affords employees the right to work in an environment free from discriminatory intimidation, ridicule, and insult" *(Vinson,* 106 S. Ct. at 2405), an employer is liable for failing to remedy known hostile or offensive work environments. *See, e.g., Garziano v. E.I. DuPont deNemours & Co.,* 818 F.2d 380, 388, 43 EPD ¶ 37,171 (5th Cir. 1987) *(Vinson* holds employers have an "affirmative duty to eradicate 'hostile or offensive' work environments"); *Bundy v. Jackson*, 641 F.2d 934, 947, 24 EPD ¶ 31,439 (D.C. Cir. 1981) (employer violated Title VII by failing to investigate and correct sexual harassment despite notice); *Tompkins v. Public Service Electric & Gas Co.*, 568 F.2d 1044, 1049, 15 EPD 7954 (3d Cir. 1977) (same); *Henson v. City of Dundee*, 682 F.2d 897, 905, 15 EPD ¶ 32,993 (11th Cir. 1982) (same); *Munford v. James T. Barnes & Co.*, 441 F. Supp. 459, 466, 16 EPD ¶ 8233 (E.D. Mich. 1977) (employer has an affirmative duty to investigate complaints of sexual harassment and to deal appropriately with the offending personnel; "failure to investigate gives tacit support to the discrimination because the absence of sanctions encourages abusive behavior").[38]

When an employer receives a complaint or otherwise learns of alleged sexual harassment in the workplace, the employer should investigate promptly and thoroughly. The employer should take immediate and appropriate corrective action by doing whatever is necessary to end the harassment, make the victim whole by restoring lost employment benefits or opportunities, and prevent the misconduct from recurring. Disciplinary action against the offending supervisor or employee, ranging from reprimand to discharge, may be necessary. Generally, the corrective action should reflect the severity of the conduct. *See Waltman v. International Paper Co.* 875 F.2d at 479 (appropriateness of remedial action will depend on the severity and persistence of the harassment and the effectiveness of any initial remedial steps). *Dornhecker v. Malibu Grand Prix Corp.*, 828 F.2d 307, 309–10, 44 EPD ¶ 37,557 (5th Cir. 1987) (the employer's remedy may be "assessed proportionately to the seriousness of the offense"). The employer should make follow-up inquiries to ensure the harassment has not resumed and the victim has not suffered retaliation.

Recent court decisions illustrate appropriate and inappropriate responses by employers. In *Barrett v. Omaha National Bank*, 726 F.2d 424, 33 EPD ¶ 34,132 (8th Cir. 1984), the victim informed her employer that her co-worker had talked to her about sexual activities and touched her in an offensive manner. Within four days of receiving this information,

---

[38] The employer's affirmative duty was first enunciated in cases of harassment based on race or national origin. *See, e.g., United States v. City of Buffalo*, 457 F. Supp. 612, 632–35, 18 EPD ¶ 8899 (W.D.N.Y. 1978), *modified in part*, 633 F.2d 643, 24 EPD ¶ 31,333 (2d Cir. 1980) (employer violated Title VII by failing to issue strong policy directive against racial slurs and harassment of black police officers, to conduct full investigations, and to take appropriate disciplinary action); *EEOC v. Murphy Motor Freight Lines, Inc.*, 488 F. Supp. 381, 385–86, 22 EPD ¶ 30,888 (D. Minn. 1980) (defendant violated Title VII because supervisors knew or should have known of co-workers' harassment of black employees, but took inadequate steps to eliminate it).

the employer investigated the charges, reprimanded the guilty employee, placed him on probation, and warned him that further misconduct would result in discharge. A second co-worker who had witnessed the harassment was also reprimanded for not intervening on the victim's behalf or reporting the conduct. The court ruled that the employer's response constituted immediate and appropriate corrective action, and on this basis found the employer not liable.

In contrast, in *Yates v. Avco Corp.*, 819 F.2d 630, 43 EPD ¶ 37,086 (6th Cir. 1987), the court found the employer's policy against sexual harassment failed to function effectively. The victim's first-level supervisor had responsibility for reporting and correcting harassment at the company, yet he was the harasser. The employer told the victims not to go to the EEOC. While giving the accused harasser administrative leave pending investigation, the employer made the plaintiffs take sick leave, which was never credited back to them and was recorded in their personnel files as excessive absenteeism without indicating they were absent because of sexual harassment. Similarly, in *Zabkowicz v. West Bend Co.*, 589 F. Supp. 780, 35 EPD ¶ 34,766 (E.D. Wis. 1984), co-workers harassed the plaintiff over a period of nearly four years in a manner the court described as "malevolent" and "outrageous." Despite the plaintiff's numerous complaints, her supervisor took no remedial action other than to hold occasional meetings at which he reminded employees of the company's policy against offensive conduct. The supervisor never conducted an investigation or disciplined any employees until the plaintiff filed an EEOC charge, at which time one of the offending co-workers was discharged and three others were suspended. The court held the employer liable because it failed to take immediate and appropriate corrective action.[39]

When an employer asserts it has taken remedial action, the Commission will investigate to determine whether the action was appropriate and, more important, effective. The EEOC investigator should, of course, conduct an independent investigation of the harassment claim, and the Commission will reach its own conclusion as to whether the law has been violated. If the Commission finds that the harassment has been eliminated, all victims made whole, and preventive measures instituted, the

[39] *See also Delgado v. Lehman*, 665 F. Supp. 460, 44 EPD ¶ 37,517 (E.D. Va. 1987) (employer failed to conduct follow-up inquiry to determine if hostile environment had dissipated); *Salazar v. Church's Fried Chicken, Inc.*, 44 FEP Cases 472 (S.D. Tex. 1987) (employer's policy inadequate because plaintiff, as a part-time teenage employee, could have concluded a complaint would be futile because the alleged harasser was the roommate of her store manager); *Brooms v. Regal Tube Co.*, 44 FEP Cases 1119 (N.D. Ill. 1987) (employer liable when a verbal reprimand proved ineffective and employer took no further action when informed of the harasser's persistence).

Commission normally will administratively close the charge because of the employer's prompt remedial action.[40] 3/19/90   Approved:_____
Date   R. Gaull Silberman
                                                               Vice Chairman

---

[40] For appropriate procedures, see §§ 4.4(e) and 15 of Volume I of the Compliance Manual.

Chapter 6

Resources

Equal Employment Opportunity Commission
Birmingham District Office
1900 Third Avenue, North, Suite 101
Birmingham, Alabama 35203
(205) 731-0082

Equal Employment Opportunity Commission
Phoenix District Office
4520 North Central Avenue, Suite 300
Phoenix, Arizona 85012-1848
(602) 640-5000

Equal Employment Opportunity Commission
Little Rock Area Office
320 West Capitol Avenue, Suite 621
Little Rock, Arkansas 72201
(501) 324-5060

Equal Employment Opportunity Commission
Fresno Local Office
1313 P Street, Suite 103
Fresno, California 93721
(209) 487-5793

Equal Employment Opportunity Commission
San Diego Area Office
880 Front Street, Room 45-21
San Diego, California 92188
(619) 557-6288

Equal Employment Opportunity Commission
Los Angeles District Office
3660 Wilshire Boulevard, Fifth floor
Los Angeles, California 90010
(213) 251-7278

Equal Employment Opportunity Commission
Oakland Local Office
1333 Broadway, Room 430
Oakland, California 94612
(415) 273-7588

Equal Employment Opportunity Commission
San Francisco District Office
901 Market Street, Suite 500
San Francisco, California 94103
(415) 744-6500

Equal Employment Opportunity Commission
San Jose Local Office
96 North Third Street, Suite 200
San Jose, California 95112
(408) 291-7352

Equal Employment Opportunity Commission
Denver District Office
1845 Sherman Street, Second Floor
Denver, Colorado 80203
(303) 866-1300

Equal Employment Opportunity Commission
Washington Field Office
1400 L Street NW, Suite 200
Washington, D.C. 20005
(202) 275-7377

Equal Employment Opportunity Commission
Miami District Office
1 Northeast First Street, Sixth floor
Miami, Florida 33132
(305) 536-4491

Equal Employment Opportunity Commission
Tampa Area Office
Timberlake Federal Building Annex
501 East Polk Street, Suite 1020
Tampa, Florida 33602
(813) 228-2310

Equal Employment Opportunity Commission
Atlanta District Office
75 Piedmont Avenue, NE, Suite 1100
Atlanta, Georgia 30335
(404) 331-6093

Equal Employment Opportunity Commission
Savannah Local Office
10 Whitaker Street, Suite B
Savannah, Georgia 31401
(912) 944-4234

Equal Employment Opportunity Commission
Honolulu Local Office
677 Ala Moana Blvd., Suite 404
Honolulu, Hawaii 96813
(808) 541-3120

Equal Employment Opportunity Commission
Chicago District Office
536 South Clark Street, Room 930-A
Chicago, Illinois 60605
(312) 353-2713

Equal Employment Opportunity Commission
Indianapolis District Office
46 East Ohio Street, Room 456

Indianapolis, Indiana 46204
(317) 226-7212

Equal Employment Opportunity Commission
Louisville Area Office
600 Martin Luther King Jr. Place, Room 268
Louisville, Kentucky 40202
(502) 582-6082

Equal Employment Opportunity Commission
New Orleans District Office
701 Loyola Avenue, Suite 600
New Orleans, Louisiana 70113
(504) 589-2329

Equal Employment Opportunity Commission
Baltimore District Office
111 Market Place, Suite 4000
Baltimore, Maryland 21202
(301) 962-3932

Equal Employment Opportunity Commission
Boston Area Office
1 Congress Street, Room 1001
Boston, Massachusetts 02114
(617) 565-3200

Equal Employment Opportunity Commission
Detroit District Office
477 Michigan Avenue, Room 1540
Detroit, Michigan 48226
(313) 226-7636

Equal Employment Opportunity Commission
Minneapolis Local Office
220 Second Street South, Room 108
Minneapolis, Minnesota 55401-2141
(612) 370-3330

Equal Employment Opportunity Commission
Jackson Area Office

Cross Road Building Complex
207 West Amite Street
Jackson, Mississippi 39201
(601) 965-4537

Equal Employment Opportunity Commission
Kansas City Area Office
911 Walnut Street, Tenth Floor
Kansas City, Missouri 64106
(816) 426-5773

Equal Employment Opportunity Commission
St. Louis District Office
625 N. Euclid Street, Fifth floor
St. Louis, Missouri 63108
(314) 425-6585

Equal Employment Opportunity Commission
Newark Area Office
60 Park Place, Room 301
Newark, New Jersey 07102
(201) 645-6383

Equal Employment Opportunity Commission
Albuquerque Area Office
505 Marquette, N.W., Suite 1105
Albuquerque, New Mexico 87102-2189
(505) 766-2061

Equal Employment Opportunity Commission
Buffalo Local Office
28 Church Street, Room 301
Buffalo, New York 14202
(716) 846-4441

Equal Employment Opportunity Commission
New York District Office
90 Church Street, Room 1501
New York, New York 10007
(212) 264-7161

Equal Employment Opportunity Commission
Charlotte District Office
5500 Central Avenue
Charlotte, North Carolina 28212
(704) 567-7100

Equal Employment Opportunity Commission
Greensboro Local Office
324 West Market Street, Room B-27
Post Office Box 3363
Greensboro, North Carolina 27401
(919) 333-5174

Equal Employment Opportunity Commission
Raleigh Area Office
1309 Annapolis Drive
Raleigh, North Carolina 27608-2129
(919) 856-4064

Equal Employment Opportunity Commission
Cincinnati Area Office
The Ameritrust Building
525 Vine Street, Suite 810
Cincinatti, Ohio 45202
(513) 684-2851

Equal Employment Opportunity Commission
Cleveland District Office
1375 Euclid Avenue, Room 600
Cleveland, Ohio 44115
(216) 522-2001

Equal Employment Opportunity Commission
Oklahoma City Area Office
531 Couch Drive
Oklahoma City, Oklahoma 73102
(405) 231-4911

Equal Employment Opportunity Commission
Philadelphia District Office
1421 Cherry Street, Tenth floor

Philadelphia, Pennsylvania 19102
(215) 656-7020

Equal Employment Opportunity Commission
Pittsburgh Area Office
1000 Liberty Avenue, Room 2038-A
Pittsburgh, Pennsylvania 15222
(412) 644-3444

Equal Employment Opportunity Commission
Greenville Local Office
15 South Main Street, Suite 530
Greenville, South Carolina 29601
(803) 241-4400

Equal Employment Opportunity Commission
Memphis District Office
1407 Union Avenue, Suite 621
Memphis, Tennessee 38104
(901) 722-2617

Equal Employment Opportunity Commission
Nashville Area Office
50 Vantage Way, Suite 202
Nashville, Tennessee 37228
(615) 736-5820

Equal Employment Opportunity Commission
Dallas District Office
8303 Elmbrook Drive
Dallas, Texas 75247
(214) 767-7015

Equal Employment Opportunity Commission
El Paso Area Office
The Commons Building C., Suite 103
4171 N. Mesa Street
El Paso, Texas 79902
(915) 534-6550

Equal Employment Opportunity Commission
Houston District Office
1919 Smith Street, Seventh Floor
Houston, Texas 77002
(713) 653-3320

Equal Employment Opportunity Commission
San Antonio District Office
5410 Frdericksburg Road, Suite 200
San Antonio, Texas 78229

Equal Employment Opportunity Commission
Norfolk Area Office
252 Monticello Avenue, First Floor
Norfolk, Virginia 23510
(804) 441-3470

Equal Employment Opportunity Commission
Richmond Area Office
3600 West Broad Street, Room 229
Richmond, Virginia 23230
(804) 771-2692

Equal Employment Opportunity Commission
Seattle District Office
2815 Second Avenue, Suite 500
Seattle, Washington 98121
(206) 553-0968

Equal Employment Opportunity Commission
Milwaukee District Office
310 West Wisconsin Avenue, Suite 800
Milwaukee, Wisconsin 53203
(414) 297-1111

SEXUAL HARASSMENT RESOURCE LIST

American Association of University Women
2401 Virginia Avenue, NW
Washington D.C. 20037

(202) 785-7700
Education on sexual harassment

American Bar Association
Commission on Women in the Profession
750 North Lake Shore Drive
Chicago, IL 60611
(312) 988-5668

American Civil Liberties Union
Women's Rights Project
132 West 43rd Street
New York, NY 10036
(212) 944-9800

Asian-American Legal Defense and Education Fund
99 Hudson Street
New York, NY 10013
(212) 966-5932
Legal assistance

Asian Immigrant Women Advocates
310 8th Street, Suite 301
Oakland, CA 94607
(510) 268-0192

Association of American Colleges
1818 R Street, NW
Washington, D.C. 20009
(202) 387-1300

Business and Professional Women/USA
2012 Massachusetts Avenue, NW
Washington, D.C. 20036
(202) 293-1100
Information clearinghouse on sexual harassment

Center for Women and Policy Studies
2000 P Street, NW, Suite 508
Washington, D.C. 20036
(202) 872-1770

Coalition of Labor Union Women
15 Union Square
New York, NY 10003
(212) 242-0700

Equal Employment Opportunity Commission (EEOC)
See separate list

Equal Rights Advocates
1663 Mission Street, Suite 550
San Francisco, CA 94103
(415) 621-0505

Federally Employed Women Legal and Education Fund
1400 Eye Street, NW
Washington, D.C. 20005
(202) 462-5235

Fund for the Feminist Majority
1600 Wilson Boulevard, Suite 704
Arlington, VA 22209
(703) 522-2501
Sexual Harassment Hotline

Lawyer's Committee for Civil Rights Under the Law
1400 Eye Street, NW, Suite 400
Washington, D.C. 20005
(202) 321-1212

Mexican American Legal Defense and Education Fund
(MALDEF)
1430 K Street, N.W.
Washington, D.C. 20005
(202) 628-4074

Ms. Foundation for Women
Ad Hoc Sexual Harassment Coalition
141 Fifth Avenue
New York, NY 10010
(212) 353-8580

NAACP Legal Defense and Educational Fund, Inc.
99 Hudson Street
New York, NY 10013
(212) 219-1900

National Association of Commissions for Women
c/o D.C. Commission for Women
N-354 Reeves Center
2000 14th Street, NW
Washington, D.C. 20009
(202) 628-5030

National Association for Public Interest Law
215 Pennsylvania Avenue, SE
Washington, D.C. 20003
(202) 546-9707

National Association for Women in Education
1325 18th Street, NW, Suite 210
Washington, D.C. 20036
(202) 659-9330

National Association of Working Women: 9 to 5
1224 Huson Road
Cleveland, OH 44113
(216) 566-9308
Job Problem Hotline (800) 522-0925

National Center for the Prevention and Control of Rape
National Institutes for Mental Health
5600 Fishers Lane
Rockville, MD 20852
(301) 443-3728

National Coalition Against Sexual Assault
Box 21378
Washington, D.C. 20009
(202) 483-7165

National Conference of State Legislatures Women's Network
1607 250th Avenue

Corwith, IA 50430
(515) 583-2156

National Council for Research on Women
The Sara Delano Roosevelt Memorial House
47–49 East 65 Street
New York, NY 10021
(212) 570-5001

National Employment Law Project
236 Massachusetts Avenue, NE
Washington, D.C. 20002
(202) 544-2185

NOW Legal Defense and Education Fund
National Association of Women and the Law
99 Hudson Street, 12th Floor
New York, NY 10013
(212) 925-6635

National Women's Law Center
1616 P. Street, NW
Washington, D.C. 20036
(202) 328-5160

Office of Personnel Management
1900 E Street, NW
Washington, D.C. 20415
(202) 606-1212

Pacific Resource Development Group
4044 NE 58th Street
Seattle, WA 98105
(206) 782-7015
Consulting group specializing in sexual harassment

Trial Lawyers for Public Justice
2000 P Street, NW, Suite 611
Washington, D.C. 20036
(202) 463-8600

United States Student Association
815 15th Street, NW, Suite 838
Washington, D.C. 20005
(202) 347-8772

Wider Opportunities for Women (WOW)
1325 G Street, NW
Washington, D.C. 20005
(202) 638-3143

Women Employed Institute
22 West Monroe, Suite 1400
Chicago, IL 60603
(312) 782-3902

Women Organized Against Sexual Harassment
P.O. Box 4768
Berkeley, CA 94704
(415) 642-7310

Women Students' Sexual Harassment Caucus
Department of Applied Psychology
Ontario Institute for Studies in Education
252 Bloor Street West
Toronto, Ontario M5S 1V6

Women's Action for Good Employment Standards (WAGES)
c/o Institute for Research on Women's Health
1616 18th Street, NW #109B
Washington, D.C. 20009
(202) 483-8643

Women's Law Project
125 South 9th Street, Suite 401
Philadelphia, PA 19107
(215) 928-9801

Women's Legal Defense Fund
1875 Connecticut Avenue, NW, Suite 710
Washington, D.C. 20009
(202) 986-2600

SELECTED, ANNOTATED BIBLIOGRAPHY ON SEXUAL HARASSMENT IN THE WORKPLACE

Books and Reports

(Unless otherwise indicated, materials are available in bookstores)

American Federation of State, County and Municipal Employees (AFSCME), *On the Job Sexual Harassment: What the Union Can Do,* (AFSCME: Washington, D.C.), 1983.

This guide reviews the various strategies presently being used to combat on the job sexual harassment and assesses their effectiveness. Possible union responses to sexual harassment are discussed and evaluated. The guide also contains a resource bibliography. To obtain a copy, contact the above organization at 1108 K Street NW, 2nd Floor, Washington, D.C. 20005. (202) 757-1756.

Baxter, Ralph, *Sexual Harassment in the Workplace: A Guide to the Law,* Revised, (Executive Enterprises Publications: New York, NY), 1985.

This book examines sexual harassment and the laws in the light of case histories and various policy statements. Some of the areas explored are the definition of sexual harassment, liability issues, mixed motive problems and limits for employer exposure to sexual harassment claims. Sample policy statements, selected resources and the Equal Employment Opportunity Commission (EEOC) guidelines on sex discrimination are included. $9.95.

California Commission on the Status of Women, *Help Yourself: A Manual for Dealing With Sexual Harassment,* (California Commission on the Status of Women: Sacramento, CA), 1987.

This manual provides information on specific actions to take when sexual harassment occurs. Legal procedures and less formal actions to stop sexual harassment are described. Free. To obtain a copy, contact the above agency at the Sexual Harassment Employment Project, 926 J Street, Room 1500, Sacramento, CA 95814. (916) 445-3173.

Center for Women in Government (CWG), *Sexual Harassment: A Digest of Landmark and Other Significant Cases,* (CWG: Albany, NY), 1988.

This digest, focusing primarily on New York cases, updates compilations of the Center's Sexual Harassment Prevention Project. The collection provides an overview of major decisions. It illustrates the variety of work settings in which sexual harassment can occur, and the range of behavior involved. The digest reviews complaint procedures, employer liability and describes the advantages of filing complaints under Title VII, tort and contract law. $10. To obtain a copy, contact the above organization at Draper Hall, 1400 Washington Avenue, Albany, NY 12222. (518) 455-6211.

Bureau of National Affairs (BNA) Inc., *Corporate Affairs: Nepotism, Office Romance, and Sexual Harassment,* (BNA, Inc.: Washington, D.C.), 1988.

This report contains analyses of research findings, trends, statutes and court decisions involving the issues of nepotism, office romance and sexual harassment. $75.00. To obtain a copy, write to the above organization's Circulation Department at P.O. Box 40947, Washington, D.C. 20077-4928.

Gutek, Barbara, *Sex and the Workplace: The Impact of Sexual Behavior and Harassment on Women, Men and Organizations,* (Jossey-Bass: San Francisco, CA), 1985.

The author presents the finding that men's and women's views on what behavior constitutes sexual harassment are generally quite different. She also found that the more "sexually charged" women perceived their workplace to be, the less job satisfaction they found. $21.95. Available in bookstores or by contacting the publisher at 350 Sansome Street 94104. (415) 433-1767.

Institute for Research on Women's Health, *Sexual Harassment and Employment Discrimination Against Women: A Consumer Handbook for Women Who Are Harmed and For Those Who Care,* (The Feminist Institute Clearinghouse: Bethesda, MD), 1988.

This guide contains information on the myths and facts of sexual harassment, the complaint process and predictable consequences of filing an administrative or legal complaint, medical and emotional aspects of employment discrimination and critical legal aspects of sexual harassment. $5.50. To obtain a copy, contact the above organization at P.O. Box 30563, Bethesda, MD 20814. (301) 951-9040.

MacKinnon, Catherine, *Sexual Harassment of Working Women: A Case of Sex Discrimination,* (Yale University Press: New Haven, CT), 1979.

This classic book examines legal questions arising from employment patterns and practices of sexual harassment and the application of the Equal Protection Clause as a remedy. Insights into the effect of sexual harassment on women. $36, $10.95.

New York City Women's Advisors Committee on Preventing Sexual Harassment, "Preventing Sexual Harassment in the Workplace: A Guide to Resource Materials," (NYC Commission on the Status of Women: New York, NY), 1987.

A helpful resource guide for those investigating sexual harassment complaints, counseling sexual harassment victims and developing or presenting sexual harassment awareness training programs. Free. To obtain a copy, contact the above agency at 52 Chambers Street, Suite 207, New York, NY 10007. (212) 566-3830.

Omilian, Susan, *Sexual Harassment in Employment,* (Callaghan and Company: Deerfield, IL), 1988.

This book presents a practical, working knowledge of what constitutes sexual harassment and when an employer is liable. It discusses how cases are initiated and contains a survey of other legal theories that may be used, such as assault and battery, the tort of outrage, right to privacy and more. $24.95. To order a copy, contact the above publisher at 155 Pfingsten Road, Deerfield, IL 60015-9917. (800) 323-1336. In Illinois, call (800) 624-8525.

Personnel Policies Forum, "Sexual Harassment: Employer Policies and Problems," (BNA, Inc.: Washington, D.C.), 1987.

This survey report presents a detailed examination of policies and procedures on sexual harassment, education and training programs and the experiments of organizations with complaints of sexual harassment. $30 plus shipping and handling. To obtain a copy, contact the above organization's Distribution and Customer Service Center, 9435 Key West Avenue, Rockville, MD 20850-3397. (301) 258-1033 or (800) 372-1033.

Wise, Sue and Liz Stanley, *Georgie Porgie: Sexual Harassment in Everyday Life,* (Pandora Press: New York, NY), 1987.

This book expands the definition of sexual harassment to mean all unwanted and intrusive behavior of men towards women. The actions are sexual in the sense that one sex, male, oppresses another sex, female. This book examines sexual harassment in a broader context than the workplace. $10.95.

Legal and General Subject Articles

Anderson, Katherine, "Employer Liability Under Title VII for Sexual Harassment After *Meritor Savings Bank vs. Vinson,*" 87 *Columbia Law Review* 1258 (1987).

This article gives an explanation of quid pro quo sexual harassment, hostile environment sexual harassment, and non-sex Title VII precedents. The positions of the District of Columbia Circuit, the EEOC, and the Supreme Court on employer liability in the case are presented. The idea of vicarious liability is also explained.

Bennett-Alexander, Dawn, "The Supreme Court Finally Speaks on the Issue of Sexual Harassment: What Did It Say?" 10 (1) *Women's Rights Law Reporter* 65, 1987.

This article gives a detailed description of the *Meritor Savings Bank vs. Vinson* case. The decisions of the District Court, the D.C. Circuit Court of Appeals and the U.S. Supreme Court with respect to the issues of quid pro quo and hostile environment harassment, voluntariness, and employer liability for supervisory employees are analyzed.

Carothers, Suzanne and Peggy Crull, "Contrasting Sexual Harassment in Female- and Male-Dominated Occupations," In *My Troubles Are Going To Have Troubles With Me,* eds. Dorothy Nemy and

Karen Bodkin Sachs, (Rutgers State University: New Jersey), 1984.

The authors have studied the differences in the forms of sexual harassment in both "traditional" and "non-traditional" jobs for women. Possible reasons for the differences are offered.

Cook, Alberta, "The New Bias Battleground: Sex Harassment," 8 *The National Law Journal,* p. 1, July 7, 1986.

This article describes the increase in sexual harassment awareness in employers and the increased number of victims who are coming forward with their complaints. There is a listing and brief summary of sexual harassment litigation.

Krieger, Linda and Cindi Fox, "Evidentiary Issues in Sexual Harassment Litigation," 1 (1) *Berkeley Women's Law Journal,* 115, Fall 1985.

This article deals with the issues of inquiry into the prior sexual conduct of a harassment victim and whether a sexual harassment victim can introduce evidence regarding the harasser's conduct toward other employees. The article concludes that in the first instance the information is not admissible in court and that in the second the information is essential to the case.

Machlowitz, David and Marilyn Machlowitz, "Preventing Sexual Harassment," *ABA Journal,* October 1, 1987.

This article provides a general overview of sexual harassment violations common in today's workplace and provides a process by which any employer can minimize the occurrence of sexual harassment in the workplace. The article also provides relevant case citations.

Manley, Marisa, "Dealing With Sexual Harassment," *INC.,* p. 146, May 1987.

This article contains suggestions for employers about what they can do to prevent sexual harassment from occurring in their companies.

McGrath, Anne, "The Touchy Issue of Sexual Harassment," *Savvy,* p. 18, April 1987.

This article is directed toward managers and what they can do to prevent sexual harassment. Suggestions on formulating a coherent policy and dealing with complaints are given.

Merriman, Christine and Cora Yang, "Employer Liability for Co-worker Sexual Harassment Under Title VII," XIII *New York University Review of Law and Social Change* 83, 1984–1985.

This article argues in favor of bringing co-worker sexual harassment cases under Title VII. The article proposes that standards of proof in co-worker sexual harassment cases are too high and that the kinds of relief granted injured co-workers are not sufficient.

Patze, John and Sandra Schermerhorn, "Sexual Harassment: Should Employers be Liable for the Damage?" *Women in Business,* p. 16-17, March/April 1987.

This article presents two opposing arguments on the issue; one on an employer's liability for sexual harassment.

Rubinett, Lynn, "Sex and Economics: The Tie That Binds—Judicial Approaches to Sexual Harassment as a Title VII Violation," IV (2) *Law and Inequality: A Journal of Theory and Practice,* 245, July 1986.

This article criticizes the two-type model of sexual harassment, quid pro quo and environmental harassment, and the inadequacy of the judicial system in addressing both the social and economic aspects of sexual harassment.

Saltzman, Amy, "Hands Off at the Office," *U.S. News and World Report,* p. 56, August 1, 1988.

This article provides information on how a victim can attempt to stop sexual harassment and/or to proceed with a formal complaint. Statistics on how women react to sexual harassment and what men and women feel constitutes sexual harassment are presented.

Journal articles can be found in legal periodicals at law libraries, law schools, courthouses and local bar associations.

Other Resources

Center for Women in Government, "Know Your Rights" (CWG: Albany, NY) 1987.

This collection of four pamphlets is a guide for women explaining their legal rights in sexual harassment situations. $2.50. To obtain copies, contact the Center at University of Albany, Draper Hall, Room 302, 1400 Washington Avenue, Albany, NY 12222. (518) 442-3900.

Community Action Strategies to Stop Rape, *Confrontation Strategies: Wall Chart,* #008 (The Feminist Institute Clearinghouse: Bethesda, MD).

This chart, originally designed for use in rape prevention programs, provides women with new responses to sexual harassment. $5.20. To obtain a copy, contact the above organization at P.O. Box 30563, Bethesda, MD 20814. (301) 951-9040.

Connecticut Women's Educational and Legal Fund (CWEALF), "Sexual Harassment in the Workplace," (CWEALF, Inc.: Hartford, CT), 1988.

This booklet provides basic information about what sexual harassment is, as well as legal information to help those who are experiencing it. $3. To obtain a copy, contact the above organization at 22 Maple Avenue, Hartford, CT 06114. (203) 247-6090.

Equal Employment Opportunity Commission (EEOC) "Guidelines on Sexual Harassment," (EEOC: Washington, D.C.).

These guidelines provide the classic definition of sexual harassment. To obtain a copy, as well as other agency directories, contact the above agency's Publications Unit, at 2401 E Street NW, Washington, D.C. 20507. (202) 634-1947.

Haimes Associates, Inc., *Sexual Harassment: A Handbook For Managers And Supervisors,* (Haimes Associates, Inc.: Philadelphia, PA).

This booklet presents relevant federal and state laws and descriptions of the latest cases, and outlines what companies must do to prevent sexual harassment. $2. To obtain a copy, contact the above organization at 708 South Washington Square, Philadelphia, PA 19106. (215) 922-1617.

New York City Commission on the Status of Women, "Sexual Harassment in the Workplace," (New York City Commission on the Status of Women: New York, NY), 1981.

A brochure informing city employees about sexual harassment in the workplace and how to prevent and combat it. Free. To obtain a copy, contact the above organization at 52 Chambers Street, Suite 207, New York, NY 10007. (212) 566-3830.

9 to 5: National Association of Working Women, "The New 9 to 5 Office Worker Survival Guide," (9 to 5: National Association of Working Women: Cleveland, OH), 1987.

This pamphlet contains information on how to evaluate office problems to make sure your rights are protected. There is a section on how to stop sexual harassment. Free. To obtain a copy, contact the above organization at 614 Superior Avenue NW, Cleveland, OH 44113. (216) 566-9308.

Robison, Ann, "Sexual Harassment Project: Local Plan," (Texas National Organization for Women (NOW): Austin, TX), 1988.

This packet, prepared by the Texas NOW Sexual Harassment Task Force, is a model for groups designing a project to deal with sexual harassment. Included are a legal definition of sexual harassment, an outline and description of laws and procedures to deal with it and suggestions on how to help the sexual harassment victim. $5. To obtain a copy, contact the above organization at P.O. Box 1256, Austin, TX 78767. (512) 458-7340.

Southeast Women's Employment Coalition, "Fact Pack," (Southeast Women's Employment Coalition: Lexington, KY), 1988.

This packet contains information on sex discrimination in employment, particularly sexual harassment. $2. To obtain a copy, write to the above organization at 382 Longview Drive, Lexington, KY 40503.

The Commonwealth of Massachusetts Commission Against Discrimination (MCAD), "The Massachusetts Commission Against Discrimination," (MCAD: Boston, MA), 1988.

This pamphlet describes the Massachusetts regulations against sex and other types of discrimination. There is a brief description of the commission's position on sexual harassment. Free. To obtain a copy, contact the above Commission at One Ashburton Place, Room 601, Boston, MA 02108. (617) 727-3990.

Women in the Workforce, "Working Women Should Know About Sexual Harassment," (Women in the Workforce: High Point, NC), 1985.

This booklet discusses the economic and physical effects of sexual harassment on women. It presents options for harassed workers on how to deal with sexual harassment. $ .75. To obtain a copy, contact the above organization at P.O. Box 2234, 842 South Main Street, High Point, NC 27261. (919) 882-0109.

TRAINING RESOURCES FOR EMPLOYERS

Anderson-Davis
1300 A 12th Avenue
San Francisco, CA 94122
(415) 661-4040
    or
424 South Newark Way
Aurora, CO 80012
(303) 360-6584

Anderson-Davis is an education service and consulting company specializing in the areas of sexual harassment/employment discrimination prevention. They have training programs to help employers learn about the issue of sexual harassment and how to deal with it in their companies.

Bureau of National Affairs Inc., Communications Center
9439 Key West Avenue
Rockville, MD 20850-3396
(800) 233-6067

BNA has a five-unit, video-based program entitled "Preventing

Sexual Harassment." The program provides a clear definition of sexual harassment and its legal implications for organizations, explores sexual harassment issues as they relate to working relationships within organizations and examines immediate and long-term preventive solutions. $875. One week rental: $310. 24-hour rental: $40. "Intent v. Impact" is an additional video training program that shows managers how to recognize and how to resolve sexual harassment in their workplaces. $850 includes 20 participant booklets and a trainers' manual.

Center for Women in Government
University at Albany
Draper Hall Room 302
1400 Washington Avenue
Albany, NY 12222
(518) 442-3900

The Center provides sexual harassment prevention training workshops to employers and their organizations. Information on how to identify, prevent and manage sexual harassment incidents is taught. To obtain a brochure or more information contact the center.

Coronet/MTI Film and Video
108 Wilmot Road
Deerfield, IL 60015
(800) 621-2131

This organization has developed two videos dealing with sexual harassment. The first, entitled "Making Advances: What Organizations Must Do About Sexual Harassment," shows how everyone from top management to line supervisors can establish and maintain a harassment-free work environment. $600. rental: $125. The second, "How Far Is Too Far?" explores recent court decisions on sexual harassment. $275. rental: $75.

Haimes Associates, Inc.
708 South Washington Square
Philadelphia, PA 99106
(215) 922-1617

This organization holds seminars on avoiding employer liability for discrimination under the state laws of New York, New Jersey and Connecticut. Along with other sex discrimination issues sexual harassment is discussed. A handbook for managers and supervisors is also available. (See *Other Resources*—Haimes Associates, Inc.).

J.M. Glasc, Inc.
P.O. Box 9999
Spokane, WA 99209-9985
(509) 326-4989

Glasc, Inc. has developed a training package entitled "Sexual Harassment is Bad Business." The package includes a 22-minute video plus a comprehensive training guide. Five-day rental: $45. Free copy of the training guide.

Learning International
Sexual Harassment Awareness Program
200 First Stamford Place
P.O. Box 10211
Stamford, CT 06904
(203) 965-8400

This organization presents a half-day program with written background materials and exercises, case histories and a video on sexual harassment.

NOW Legal Defense and Education Fund
99 Hudson Street
12th floor
New York, NY 10013
(212) 925-6635

This organization's video training program, *Sexual Harassment: Walking the Corporate Fine Line,* focuses on the *Meritor Savings Bank v. Vinson* U.S. Supreme Court decision and its impact on employer liability. Legal definitions of what actions constitute employer liability are included. The basics of developing and communicating an effective policy are presented. Includes program workbook. Indicate VHS 1/2″ or 3/4″ format. Rental: $100.

Index

agency, principles of, 135, 142, 164, 178–182, 186

Alexander v. Gardner-Denver Co., 181*n*

Alexander v. Yale, 28–29

Alicia Rosado v. Garcia Santiago, 140

American Bar Association, 126

"American Lawyer: When and How to Use One, The" (ABA), 126

American Management Association, 70

Anderson v. Methodist Evangelical Hospital, Inc., 179*n*

anti-harassment policies, 70–71, 76, 97, 102–103, 122, 152–158, 180, 183–184, 186
  of Harvard University, 108–114
  as preventive measures, 152–153
  in schools, 108–116, 118
  of University of Iowa, 114–116

apparent authority, 183–185

Arnold v. City of Seminole, 144

ASME v. Hydrolevel, 142

assault, 23, 120, 121, 128, 145, 174

attorneys:
  advice of, 68, 88, 120–121
  and EEOC complaints, 79, 124, 125
  fees of, 68, 90, 125, 126
  in private lawsuits, 80
  sources of, 126–127

Barbetta v. Chemlawn Services Corp., 137, 176

Barnes v. Costle, 27, 132, 141, 161*n*, 165

Barrett v. Omaha National Bank, 174, 181*n*, 187

Belanoff v. Grayson, 146

Bell v. Crackin Good Bakers, Inc., 134

Bennett v. Corroon & Black Corp., 137, 176

"bi–sexual supervisor" defense, 141

Bohen v. City of East Chicago, 139, 144

boss–secretary relationships, 50

Bouchet v. National Urban League, 133

Bourque v. Powell Electrical Mfg. Co., 140, 177

Broderick v. Ruder, 86–87, 137, 162*n*

Broderick v. Shad, 148

Brooms v. Regal Tube Co., 140, 182*n*, 185, 188*n*

Bundy v. Jackson, 132, 161*n*, 171*n*, 187

burden of proof, *see* proof of harm

Bureau of National Affairs (BNA), 141

California, University of, 109

Cariddi v. Kansas Chiefs Football Club, Inc., 137

Carrero v. New York City Housing Authority, 140

Carroll v. Talman Federal Savings & Loan Association, 134, 136

case law, 90, 92–93, 100
  EEOC Guidelines and, 160–189

as guidance for counsel, 131*n*
in training programs, 102
character, defamation of, 76
charges, *see* complaints
Civil Rights Act (1866), 144
Civil Rights Act (1964), Title VII of,
    see Title VII of Civil Rights Act
Civil Rights Act (1991), 63
damages limited under, 91, 125–126
claims, *see* complaints
Clark v. Marash, 177
Clark v. World Airways, 145
"class claims," 82
Cody v. Marriott Corp., 148
"coerced caring," 50–51
coercion, 66, 128
colleges, *see* schools
Collins v. Pfizer, Inc., 148
comments, sexually suggestive, 22–24,
    65, 66, 84, 85, 121, 128, 161*n*,
    175–176
complaints:
    alternate avenues of, 154, 155–156
    confidentiality of, 67, 69, 71, 81,
        113, 155
    contents of, 88, 123, 124, 143, 153
    costs of, 123, 125
    with EEOC, 67, 68, 72, 77–81, 87,
        88, 123, 167
    evidence needed in, 88, 122, 123
    of federal employees, 103–106, 143
    informal resolution of, 104, 106,
        113, 122–123, 153–154
    internal consistency in, 170
    investigation of, *see* investigations
    lawsuits and, 71, 74, 79–82, 122,
        166
    limited effect of, 46–48
    procedures for, 67, 68, 71, 105–
        106, 113–114, 122–124, 143–
        144, 153–154
    questions about, 124
    resolution of, 69, 71, 123
    retaliation and reprisals as result of,
        see retaliation, reprisals
    in schools, 113–114
    timeliness of, 67, 69, 79, 89, 104,
        106, 107, 124, 143–144, 166–167
    in writing, 88, 123–124

confidentiality:
    EEOC and, 81
    grievance procedures and, 71, 122
    lawsuits and, 81
    victims' concerns about, 67, 69, 71,
        81, 113
    as victims' right, 102, 155
consensual relationships, 18, 63, 66,
    84
    lawsuits and, 133, 163–164, 184
    in schools, 109, 111–112, 114–116,
        118
    unwelcomeness vs., 163–169
constructive discharge, 74, 139–140,
    152, 162, 167, 177–178, 182*n*,
    184
"Corporate Affairs: Nepotism, Office
    Romance and Sexual
    Harassment," 141
corroboration, *see* evidence; witnesses
costs:
    of complaints, 82, 123–124, 125
    federal funding for, 125
    of lawsuits, 90, 123, 126
    sharing of, 123
    to society, 15–16, 98
courts:
    complex procedures in, 125
    evidence required by, 158
    monetary awards by, 91
    time limits in, 143–144
    Title VII and, 82–83
    see also lawsuits
Cummings v. Walsh Construction Co.,
    138

damages:
    caps on, 91, 125–126
    compensatory, 83, 91, 125
    emotional, 81, 92, 174*n*
    monetary, 76, 81, 87, 91, 117, 125–
        126, 174*n*
    punitive, 83, 91, 125
    under state laws, 126
Davis v. Monsanto Chemical Co., 138
*De Cintio v. Westchester County
    Medical Center,* 141, 162*n*
defamation of character, 76
Delgado v. Lehman, 134, 149, 188*n*

Derr v. Gulf Oil Corp., 177
discharge:
  constructive, 74, 139–140, 152,
    162, 167, 177–178, 182*n,* 184
  retaliatory, 162, 167
  wrongful, 76, 81, 87, 174*n*
disciplinary action, 70, 110, 113, 156
disparate treatment, definition of, 134
*Dornhecker v. Malibu Grand Prix
    Corp.,* 178, 187
Dothard v. Rawlinson, 134
*Downes v. Federal Aviation
    Administration,* 173*n*

educational institutions, *see* schools
Education Amendments Act (1972),
    Title IX of, *see* Title IX of
    Education Amendments Act
education and training, 71, 76, 97,
    99, 101–102, 155
Education Department, Office of Civil
    Rights for, 116, 118, 145
EEOC (Equal Employment
    Opportunity Commission), U.S.:
  complaints filed with, 68, 72, 74,
    77–82, 87, 88, 123–124, 181–182
  confidentiality and, 81
  fees and, 82, 123, 125
  investigations by, 77, 79–81, 106–
    107, 124, 169–171
  lawsuits and, 77, 78, 79, 80–81,
    124–125
  legal protection by, 77–78
  local offices of, 191–198
  Meritor and, 78, 83, 163
  procedures of, 72, 74, 88–89, 124
  purposes of, 77
  Review and Appeals Department of,
    106, 107
  "right to sue" letter of, 80, 81–82,
    124–125
  time limits of, 124
EEOC Guidelines, 77, 79–82, 94,
    160–189
  employers' reliance on, 70
  hostile environment described in,
    78, 85, 94, 128–129
  lawsuits and, 77, 78, 80–81, 100,
    160–189

  on nepotism, 141
  quid pro quo cases and, 78, 128,
    169
  schools and, 117
  sexual harassment defined in, 63,
    94, 102, 128–129, 131, 151, 160–
    165
  Supreme Court ruling and, 164–
    165
*EEOC v. Board of Governors of State
    Colleges & Universities,* 182*n*
*EEOC v. Federal Reserve Bank of
    Richmond,* 177
EEOC v. Hacienda Hotel, 183
*EEOC v. Murphy Motor Freight Lines,
    Inc.,* 187*n*
Elliott v. Emery Air Freight, 30
employers, 70–76
  actions required of, 72–74, 121,
    137, 160, 166*n,* 181, 182
  agents of, 135, 142, 164, 178–182,
    186
  anti–harassment policies of, 70–71,
    76, 97, 102–103, 122, 152–158,
    180, 183–184, 186
  employment practices of, 87, 160
  employment records of, 123, 158
  Equal Employment Opportunity
    counselors and, 105–106
  federal agencies as, 88, 92–107,
    141, 142
  grievance procedures of, 70, 71, 72,
    75, 76, 122, 153–154, 177, 180–
    184, 186
  investigations by, 73–74, 122, 123,
    166*n,* 181
  and knowledge of hostile
    environment, 75, 76, 90, 122,
    139, 142, 157, 163, 164, 180–186
  liability of, *see* liability
  non-employees and, 75
  notification of, 74, 79, 121–122,
    124–125, 142–143, 165, 175*n,*
    178, 181, 182*n*
  options of, 72
  and organization size, 77–79, 125–
    126, 141, 144
  victims' lawsuits against, 74, 80–82,
    90, 122

see also schools

equal employment laws, 88, 120–121
  damages available under, 125–126
  rights protected by, 14, 121–123, 126, 135, 136, 152, 166, 174, 186
  state and local administration of, 123–124
  time limits under, 143, 154
Equal Employment Opportunity Commission, see EEOC, U.S.
Equal Employment Opportunity counselors, 105–106
evidence:
  in complaints, 88, 122, 123
  corroborative, 72, 89, 169–171
  in investigations, 156, 166, 167, 169–171
  nature of, 170
Executive Order 11246, 145

"facial" discrimination, 134
federal agencies:
  anti-harassment policy statements by, 102–103
  complaint and investigation procedures of, 97, 99, 103–105, 106, 123–125
  EEOC hearings and, 106–107
  as employers, 88, 92–107, 141, 142
  prevention efforts in, 104–105
federal funding:
  for legal costs, 125
  of schools, 83, 118
fees:
  of attorneys, 90
  contingency, 68, 125, 126
  EEOC and, 82, 123, 125
  of state and local agencies, 123–124
Ferguson v. E.I. DuPont deNemours & Co., 168n, 181n
Fields v. Horizon House, Inc., 182, 183n, 184n, 185
Flowers v. Crouch-Walker Corp., 179n
Ford v. Revlon, Inc., 145
Freedman v. American Standard, 173n

Gan v. Kepro Circuit Systems, 168

Garziano v. E.I. DuPont deNemours & Co., 186
General Electric Co. v. Gilbert, 164n
Gilardi v. Schroeder, 174n
Goss v. Exxon Office Systems Co., 177
Great American Savings & Loan v. Novotny, 144
grievance procedures, 70, 72, 75, 76, 153–154
  confidentiality of, 71, 122
  employer's liability and, 177, 180–184, 186
  in schools, 108, 116–117, 118
  of unions, 45–46, 123
  "Guidance for Advocates," 122, 151–158

Hall v. F. O. Thacker Co., 170n
Hall v. Gus Construction Co., 174, 177
harassers:
  behavior of, 85, 95
  co-workers as, 65, 75, 85, 90, 96, 121, 124
  credibility of, 166, 169
  gender of, 64, 162
  in hostile environment complaints, 129
  interviews of, 73, 89, 169
  multiple targets of, 157–158
  penalties and sanctions against, 99, 101, 103, 113, 153, 156, 186
  power abused by, 14–15, 112, 115–116, 128
  in quid pro quo complaints, 129, 135
  and requests to stop harassment, 68, 96–97, 108, 121, 122, 129–131, 162, 166, 169
  school staff and faculty as, 108, 109, 111, 114–115, 117–118
  supervisors as, 75, 90, 94–95, 96, 104, 121, 124, 129, 132, 154, 161, 164, 178–186
  typical, 69
harassment, see sexual harassment
Harvard University, anti-harassment policy statement of, 108–114
hearings after investigations, 106–107

Held v. Gulf Oil Co., 177
Henson v. City of Dundee, 134, 135, 139, 181, 187
  corroborative evidence in, 169*n*
  hostile environment defined in, 136, 138, 161*n*, 165, 172
  unwelcome behavior defined in, 165–166
Hicks v. Gates Rubber Co., 134, 174, 176, 177, 185, 186
Highlander v. K.F.C. National Management Co., 173
Hill, Anita, 12–16
histories:
  psychological, 92, 147–148
  sexual, 92, 147
Hollis v. Fleetguard, Inc., 173*n*
Hopkins v. Price Waterhouse, 140
hostile environment, 34–42, 63, 75, 83, 84–86, 122
  agency principles in, 180–182
  behavior patterns in, 34–35, 39–40, 85, 86, 173–175
  constructive discharge and, 177–178
  definitions of, 132, 136, 138, 161*n*, 164–165, 171–172, 176
  EEOC Guidelines and, 78, 85, 94, 128–129
  Meritor and, 83, 86, 136, 138, 161, 163–164
  nature of, 171–172, 175–177
  physical harassment in, 174
  pornography in, 85, 121, 175
  proof of harm in, 135–138, 174*n*
  quid pro quo and, 129, 132, 162, 173–174, 186
  "reasonable person" and, 137, 139, 173–174
  retaliation and reprisals in, 132
  in settings where women were previously excluded, 138
  sexual comments in, 85, 161*n*, 175–176
  third parties in, 86–87, 137, 162*n*, 174
  Title VII and, 83
  unwelcome sexual behavior in, 84–85, 129, 136–138, 173–176

Huddleston v. Roger Dean Chevrolet, 135, 140
human rights agencies, *see* state agencies
Hunter v. Allis-Chalmers Corp., 181*n*, 182

In re Mitchell, 147
investigations:
  by EEOC, 77, 79–81, 106–107, 124, 169–171
  by employers, 73–74, 122, 123, 166*n*, 181
  evidence important in, 166, 167, 169–171
  by federal agencies, 97, 99, 103–104, 106
  interviews in, 73, 89, 169, 170
  nature of, 88–89, 157, 162
  procedures for, 71, 73, 76, 79–82, 106–107, 156–158
  results of, 80, 106, 124–125
  by state and local agencies, 124
  timeliness of, 79
  by unbiased investigators, 156–157
  witnesses in, 106
Iowa, University of, anti-harassment policy statement of, 114–116
I.U.O.E. v. Robbins & Myers, Inc., 182*n*

Jones v. Flagship International, 149, 174

Katz v. Dole, 133, 139, 161*n*, 168–169
King v. Palmer, 141, 162*n*
Kremer v. Chemical Construction Corp., 144
Kyriazi v. Western Electric Co., 145

Law of Workmen's Compensation, The (Larson), 146
laws:
  common, 145–146
  criminal, 87
  equal employment, *see* equal employment laws
  personal injury, 120

Index

sexual discrimination, 120–121
on torts, 126, 135, 145–146, 147
workers' compensation, 88, 120
lawsuits:
compensation and damages in, 87, 91
complaints and, 71, 74, 79–82, 123, 143–144, 163, 166
co-plaintiffs in, 123
costs of, 90, 123, 126
against co–workers, 90, 122
by EEOC, 79, 80, 125
EEOC Guidelines and, 77, 78, 80, 100, 160–189
against employers, 122–123
by federal employees, 107
grievance procedures and, 123
of hostile environment cases, 75, 84–85, 90, 163–164
out-of-court settlement of, 69
of quid pro quo cases, 75, 84, 90
"reasonable person" as standard in, 121, 136, 137, 140
"right to sue" letters and, 80, 81–82, 125
and size of company, 77–79
by students, 117, 118
third parties in, 162n
time span of, 69, 107
by victims, 80–82, 125, 163
lawyers, *see* attorneys
Legal Aid Society, 125
Legal Services Corporation, 125
liability:
direct, 180–182
of employer, 73, 91, 125–126, 135, 137, 139, 142–143, 160–165, 174n, 177n, 178–185
imputed, 182–183
limits of, 75–76
Lipsett v. University of Puerto Rico, 138, 166n, 173, 179, 181
litigation, *see* lawsuits
Llewellyn v. Celanese Corp., 138
Loftin-Boggs v. City of Meridian, 169n
Lowe v. Philadelphia Newspapers, Inc., 148, 149

McKinney v. Dole, 134, 176
MacKinnon, Catherine, 19–60
Marshall, Thurgood, 72, 177
men, harassment of, 95, 128n, 141–142, 162n
Meritor Savings Bank FSB v. Vinson, 72, 78, 86, 103–104, 131, 163–164, 171, 173, 177–178, 179, 180–182, 186–187
case law developed after, 160–161
consensual relationships in, 133, 163
employers' liability in, 78, 83, 163
facts in, 163
formal notification procedures in, 143
hostile environment in, 83, 86, 136, 138, 161, 163–164
precedents set by, 83, 150, 152, 160–161, 164, 165
principles of agency in, 135
proof of harm in, 135, 139, 149
victim's speech and dress in, 146, 167
see also Vinson v. Taylor
Merit Systems Protection Board, U.S.:
purposes of, 93
recommendations of, 98–105, 116–117
study by (1980), 92–93
survey by (1987), 68, 93–107, 138
Miller v. Aluminum Company of America, 146, 162n
Miller v. Bank of America, 30, 161n
Mitchell v. Hutchings, 146–148
monetary damages, 76, 81, 87, 91, 117, 125–126, 174n
Moylan v. Maries County, 173n
Muller v. United States Steel Corp., 140
Munford v. James T. Barnes & Co., 24, 187

National Black Women's Health Project, 127
National Employment Lawyers' Association, 126
National Lawyers Guild, 127
Neidhart v. D. H. Holmes Co., 170n

nepotism, EEOC Guidelines on, 141
Neville v. Taft Broadcasting Co., 174*n*
Nolan v. Cleland, 177
non-employees, employers' liability and, 75
notification:
  of employer, 74, 79, 121–122, 124–125, 142–143, 165, 175*n*, 178, 181, 182*n*
  of harasser, 68, 96–97, 108, 121, 122, 129–131, 162, 166, 169
  of harasser's supervisor, 122
  of safeguard legal claims, 122
  of victim's supervisor, 122
NOW (National Organization for Women), Legal Defense and Education Fund of, 127

Office of Civil Rights for the Department of Education, 116, 118, 145
O'Reilly v. Executone of Albany, Inc., 145

Pease v. Alford Photo Industries, Inc., 136, 145
Phillips v. Martin Marietta, 134
policies, anti-harassment,
see anti-harassment policies
"Policy Guidance on Employer Liability Under Title VII for Sexual Favoritism," 162*n*
pornography, 85, 121, 175
Porta v. Rollins Environmental Services, Inc., 137
power, abuse of, 14, 15, 38, 112, 115–116, 129, 162, 183
preventive and remedial action, 70, 101, 104–105, 152–153, 161, 186–188
Price Waterhouse v. Hopkins, 134
Priest v. Rotary, 141, 147
proof of harm, 89, 132, 133, 134–135, 139, 142–143, 149, 174*n*
  in hostile environment cases, 135–138
  in quid pro quo cases, 135
psychological history, 92, 147–148

quid pro quo harassment, 26–34, 63, 66, 75, 76, 121, 151
  agency principles in, 179–180
  in *Barnes v. Costle,* 132
  behavior patterns in, 40–41, 84
  constructive discharge in, 177–178
  EEOC Guidelines and, 78, 128, 169
  employer liability and, 179–180
  hostile environment and, 129, 132, 162, 173–174, 186
  proof of harm in, 135, 174*n*
  in schools, 117
  third parties denied benefits in, 86–87, 115
  victim's behavior and, 26–29, 169

Rabidue v. Osceola Refining Co., 138, 173, 175–176
  hostile environment defined in, 176
racial discrimination, sexual discrimination compared with, 24–25, 94, 137, 138, 164
rape, 41, 46, 121, 128, 163, 174*n*
"reasonable person" standard, 121, 136, 137, 139, 140, 172–174
records, written, 67, 68, 88, 106, 108, 118, 122, 123–124, 142–143, 158
Redbook Magazine survey (1976), 20–23
Reichman v. Bureau of Affirmative Action, 168*n*
resignation as "constructive discharge," 74
resources, list of, 198–214
retaliation, reprisals:
  forms of, 29–31, 46–47, 132
  as prohibited by law, 74
  as result of complaints, 46–47, 67, 122–123, 132, 154, 167
  as victims' fear, 44–45, 102, 162, 166, 183
retaliatory discharge, 162, 167
"right to sue" letter, 80, 81–82, 124–125
Robinson v. Jacksonville Shipyards, Inc., 147
Rogers v. EEOC, 137, 173
Ross v. Comsat, 172
Ross v. Double Diamond, 136

Index

Rowbotham, Sheila, 43
Ryzlak v. McNeil Pharmacy Co., 148

Safilios-Rothschild, Constantina, 31
*Salazar v. Church's Fried Chicken,
    Inc.,* 188n
Sapp v. City of Warner-Robins, 173n
*Sardigal v. St. Louis National
    Stockyards Co.,* 133, 167n, 170n
Schlagenhauf v. Holder, 147
schools, 107–118
    anti-harassment policy statements
        of, 108–116, 118
    complaint procedures in, 109, 113
    consensual relationships in, 109,
        111–112, 114–116, 118
    definition of sexual harassment in,
        112
    EEOC Guidelines and, 117
    federal funding of, 83, 118
    grievance procedures in, 108, 116–
        117, 118
    and knowledge of harassment, 118
    monetary damages and, 117
    professionalism in, 109, 111–112,
        115–116
    quid pro quo cases in, 117
    third-party complaints and, 117
    Title IX and, 83, 107, 117
Schroeder v. Schock, 135
"scope of employment," 182–183
Scott v. Sears, Roebuck and Co., 173n
"sexism," use of term, 111
sexual discrimination:
    behaviors construed as, 133–134
    harassment as form of, 19, 20–21,
        63, 64, 83, 102, 132, 151, 160,
        164–165
    racial discrimination compared
        with, 94
sexual discrimination laws, 120–121
sexual harassment:
    behavior patterns in, 21–23, 68, 69,
        85, 86, 94, 96, 102, 114, 117,
        121, 122, 157, 173n
    changing attitudes about, 93, 95,
        98, 99, 109, 110
    costs of, *see* costs

definitions of, 63, 66, 93–94, 112,
    128–129, 161
EEOC Guidelines on, *see* EEOC
    Guidelines
experience vs. legal definition of,
    19–60, 93
filing complaints of, 120
individual instances of, 121, 122
of men, 95, 128n, 141–142, 162n
nature of, 23, 63–66, 93–94, 100,
    109, 111, 112, 114–115, 117,
    120, 121, 128, 131–140, 151
pervasiveness of, 19–25
power as element in, 112, 115–116,
    129
productivity and, 152–153
resource list in, 198–214
single incidents of, 65, 86, 174
statistics on, 12–13, 66, 95, 108
use of term, 82, 93–94
victims of, *see* victims
as violation of equal employment
    rights, 121–122, 174
*Sexual Harassment and Working
    Women* (MacKinnon), 19–60
"Sexual Harassment: Employer
    Policies and Problems," 103, 149
*Sexual Harassment in the Federal
    Government: An Update,* 139
"Sexual Harassment in the Federal
    Workplace," 142
"Sexual Harassment in the Workplace
    Litigation," 127, 131–150
sexual history in lawsuits, 92, 147
sexuality, focus on, 128, 135
sexual orientation, 84, 141
Skidmore v. Swift & Co., 164n
Snell v. Suffolk County, 138
Sparks v. Pilot Freight Carriers, 135,
    179, 186
Sprogis v. United Air Lines, Inc., 138
state agencies, 87
    complaints filed with, 87–88, 123–
        124
    time limits of, 79, 124
states:
    equal employment laws in, 88
    workers' compensation laws in, 88
Studstill v. Borg Warner Leasing, 145

222

Index

support groups, 127, 150
Supreme Court, U.S., 83
    EEOC Guidelines interpreted by, 164–165
    Meritor decision of, *see Meritor Savings Bank FSB v. Vinson*
    Title IX and, 117
Swentek v. USAir, Inc., 168

Taylor v. Jones, 181
third parties:
    corroboration by, 73, 89, 123, 169, 170
    in hostile environments, 86–87, 137, 162*n*, 174
    as plaintiffs, 141
    in schools, 115, 117
    self–help measures and, 153
Tidwell v. American Oil Co., 179*n*
Title VII of Civil Rights Act (1964), 86
    courts and, 82–83
    hostile environment as violation of, 83
    injunctions under, 83
    schools and, 107
    time limits of, 181–182
Title IX of Education Amendments Act (1972):
    complaints filed under, 145
    federal funds and, 83, 107
    monetary damages under, 117
    sexual harassment as violation of, 109
Tompkins v. Public Service Electric & Gas Co., 27, 187
torts, 79–80, 90, 126, 135, 145–146, 147
Toscano v. Nimmo, 141
totality of circumstances, in defining unwelcome sexual behavior, 136, 166, 175
training and education, 70, 76, 97, 99, 101–102, 155
transfer, refusal of, 167*n*
Trial Lawyers for Public Justice, 126
Tunis v. Corning Glass Works, 137

Ukarish v. Magnesium Electron, 167*n*

unions:
    grievance procedures of, 45–46, 123
    Title IX and, 142
United States v. City of Buffalo, 187*n*
universities, *see* schools
unwelcome sexual behavior, 63–64, 66, 68, 92, 94, 100, 113, 128, 132, 151
    consensual relationships vs., 163–164, 165–169
    definitions of, 161, 165–166
    in hostile environments, 84–85, 129, 136–138, 173–176
    notification of, 121, 122, 169
    physical vs. verbal harassment in, 173–176
    in quid pro quo cases, 132–135, 169
    as threshold standard for court cases, 133, 135–136, 146–147, 161, 165–169
    totality of circumstances in, 136, 166, 175
    types of, 108, 175–177
    victims' behavior and, 167–169
    written statement of, 68
    see also consensual relationships

Vaughn v. Pool Offshore Co., 137
venue:
    outside workplace as, 65, 116
    workplace as, 63
Vermett v. Hough, 148
victims:
    actions of, 66–68, 73, 74, 80–82, 123–124, 144, 153, 167–169
    black women as, 49–50
    burden of proof with, 89, 133, 135–138, 142–143
    co-workers as, 65, 85
    credibility of, 133, 165, 166, 167, 169
    as discredited by harassers, 69
    emotional effects on, 42–48
    employers as, 65
    employers sued directly by, 76, 80–82, 90, 122, 141
    employment records of, 123, 158
    federal employees as, 92–107

Index

hesitation to report by, 13–15, 67, 163, 166, 167
interviews of, 73, 89, 169
lack of reaction by, 13, 14, 44–45, 49, 68, 96, 133, 167, 180
men as, 25, 64, 95, 128n, 141, 162n
professors as, 108
remedies available to, 87, 96–97, 102, 105, 113–114, 144
speech and dress of, 146, 147, 165
students as, 108, 109
typical, 69, 95
see also sexual harassment
Vinson v. Superior Court of Alameda County, 147, 148
Vinson v. Taylor, 149, 163–164
Volk v. Coler, 137
voluntary sexual conduct, *see* consensual relationships

Walker v. Ford Motor Co., 137, 138
Waltman v. International Paper Co., 176, 187
Wehrli, Lynn, 43–44
Williams v. Bell, 161n
Williams v. Civiletti, 161n

Williams v. Saxbe, 30, 161n
witnesses, 73, 89, 106, 123, 169, 170
women:
depressed employment status of, 35–38, 48, 49
job advancements of, 31–34
rights of, 158
as sex objects, 34
as victims of harassment, *see* victims
workers' compensation laws, 88, 120, 146
Working Woman Sexual Harassment Survey (1988), 20–24, 152–153
work performance, 63, 98, 128, 129, 152–153, 172
written records, 67, 68, 88, 106, 108, 118, 122, 123–124, 142–143, 158
wrongful discharge, 76, 81, 87, 174n

Yates v. Avco Corp., 139, 140, 142, 149, 181, 188
Young v. South Western Savings & Loan Assn., 140

Zabkowicz v. West Bend Co., 149, 172, 188